prnpls v spdr arlhn sdn TS ***

Joe M. Pullis, Ed.D.

Professor, Department of Office Administration
and Business Communication
College of Administration and Business
Louisiana Tech University

GLENCOE
McGraw-Hill
Mission Hills, California

***PRINCIPLES OF *Speedwriting*
SHORTHAND STUDENT TRANSCRIPT**

Send all inquiries to:
Glencoe
15319 Chatsworth Street
Mission Hills, California 91395-9509

Printed in the United States of America

ISBN 0-02-685110-5

  8 9 10   96 95 94

LESSON
1

**WORD
CONSTRUCTION**

abr

ln

rsv

spli

hlp

sle

lrvl

dla

ll

hld

llfn

ofr

READING AND WRITING EXERCISES

Series A

1. We hope to see you soon.
2. Will you pay a fee?
3. It is a new file unit.
4. Is the unit too tall?
5. Sue will not fly to Dallas.

Series B

1. Ed is in his office.
2. Did you receive a bill?

3. Tell Debbie to pay it.
4. You will do well in an office job.
5. We will give you a raise in pay.

Series C

1. Is Bill at the office?
2. The review is easy to type.
3. Sue will grade it.
4. Is the new budget ready to review?
5. We did not receive it.

LESSON

2

WORD DEVELOPMENT

(shorthand outlines)

WORD CONSTRUCTION

(shorthand outlines)

READING AND WRITING EXERCISES

Series A

1. Are you ready to do some typing?
2. We will help you if we can. It is our job.
3. The president and vice president of our company will see us in a week.
4. Do you have the new bulletin? It is very well written.
5. Which week are you planning to visit the office?

Series B

1. Let me know when the information arrives.
2. I will mail a full deposit.
3. You will receive a free gift for each savings deposit.

4. I will return the check to the company.
5. Here is a check to cover the fee in full.

Series C

1. We are making changes in our company catalog.

2. We will mail you a copy very soon.
3. We are attaching a copy of the bill. When can you mail us a check?
4. Bob needs to know something very soon.
5. I will leave the information at his desk.

LESSON ▮▮▮▮▮▮▮▮▮▮▮▮▮▮▮▮

3

WORD DEVELOPMENT

pa̱	*pam*	*pams*
pēNs	*pēNr*	*pēṈ*
agres	*agrē̱*	*agrem*
plss	*rpls*	*plsm*
rNl	*rṈ*	*rNr*
slls	*slḻ*	*sllms*

WORD CONSTRUCTION

evN	*mbr*
dfrN	*dcms*
asnm	*‿vm*
sNrl	*prN*
rcm	*mrẕ*
plzN	*rmbr*

READING AND WRITING EXERCISES

1

MEMO TO: Melvin Carter

I can give you information you need to make the changes in our sales plan. I[1] have a copy of the new plan which gives full details.

At the current time, our office is keeping a very busy[2] schedule. We are making plans for some big events for the weeks ahead. In case you try to reach me at my office,[3] I will leave the copies you need at the front desk.

Feel free to call me for help in the future if you need it.[4] (80)

2

MEMO TO: Judy Jackson

My memo is to remind you of our plans to hold budget hearings in the near future.[1]

The reason for the hearings is to review new budget items and the money we will need to pay for such[2] entries. We are making a schedule for each office. You will receive a notice assigning you a definite[3] time.

If you have new items or replacements, plan to give a brief summary of each at the hearing. (78)

LESSON

4

WORD DEVELOPMENT

[shorthand characters]

WORD CONSTRUCTION

[shorthand characters]

READING AND WRITING EXERCISES

1

MEMO TO: Charles Gray

Our rental buildings need repair. We should paint the walls and replace the floor coverings in each[1] room. We should also replace the washing machines in each unit.

Our leasing agent doesn't want us to raise the[2] rent. Each lease is current. She is hoping to keep the buildings full.

What is Ed's advice? I will ask the agent to[3] give you a call to set a time to show you each building. (70)

2

Dear Mrs. Chase:

We have your letter applying for a job in our firm.

Will you also mail us a letter which[1] gives us information on the typing and filing classes you have taken? We may have an opening in our[2] office soon.

For your information, we are attaching a copy of our company's hiring policies. Let[3] us know when you can visit our firm. We hope to hear from you soon. Yours truly, (74)

3

Dear Mr. Parker:

I forgot to mail my payment to your firm. I hope you will forgive the delay. Here is a[1] check covering part of the bill. I will pay the entire bill very soon. Sincerely, (35)

4

MEMO TO: Miss Sue Green

I sent an informal letter to the president of the firm asking to see a copy[1] of the new marketing report. To my knowledge, we do not yet have a reply.

Would you also remind the[2] president we would very much like to know his plans for opening our new offices? It is time to decide[3] on which furnishings we will need. We would like to have your advice too.

Let me know when you can make the trip to our[4] new plant. I shall try to see you at the office when you arrive. (91)

5

Dear Ms. Harper:

Perhaps you have not seen our new catalog. If not, will you take a few minutes to read the form[1] we are attaching? You will see we are showing many new items.

If you would like to receive a copy of[2] the catalog, sign the form and return it to our office. We will rush the catalog to you.

Many people[3] like to use our catalog to shop at home. Won't you choose the easy way to shop too? Cordially yours, (78)

6

MEMO TO: Bill Davidson

We do not have a plan for training our people to run our new machines. Perhaps the[1] plant manager and our chief engineer can help design a plan we could use for the entire company. Let us[2] know what you plan to do.

Also, will you mail us a copy of your new budget? We need to review it at[3] management planning time. Perhaps we can save money in the future if we take time to look at each part of our[4] budget. (81)

LESSON 5

WORD DEVELOPMENT

olsd	*olln*	*ollns*
rSCs	*rSC*	*rSCr*
dols	*dol*	*dolls*
Svas	*Sva*	*Svar*
aloo	*alo*	
Sprzs	*Sprz*	

WORD CONSTRUCTION

ho	*don*
rhoo	*Svss*
por	*Scl*
SC	*olfl*
ollc	*Sv*
Slfcls	*donlon*

READING AND WRITING EXERCISES

1

Dear Sue:

Can you tell me when you will finish your report on savings certificates? Bill Brown told me you are[1] making a survey. If we can, we would like to use the information in your survey in our own report. Very[2] truly yours, (42)

2

Gentlemen:

We are hoping to hold a company luncheon in your hotel soon. Can you give us information[1] on your policy for renting luncheon rooms? What services do you offer, and how many people will your rooms[2] hold? Also, what is your minimum rental fee? How much time do you allow for reserving the room?

We hope to[3] make our final plans very soon. Sincerely yours, (69)

3

Dear Joe:

I have written a letter to Gail Brown telling her we are canceling her policy. We are certain[1] to hear from her the minute she receives the letter. Perhaps we can recommend a new agent for her. Let me[2] know if you have a name to give her. Yours truly, (49)

4

Dear Sir or Madam:

Are you paying high rent and yet have very little to show for it? Perhaps you would like to[1] own your own home, yet cannot seem to save enough money for the down payment.

If so, we can help you. We are now[2] offering a new home payment plan which will allow you to place a low down payment on your new home. We also[3] have a budget plan for house payments. If you take out a loan from us now, you can schedule your payments any way[4] you wish.

Give us a minute of your time, and we will show you an easy payment plan for your household. Cordially[5] yours, (101)

5

Gentlemen:

We are returning the copying machine we bought from your firm. Sometimes the machine will not print. When[1] it does print, the copies are not clear.

We have made many calls in search of an agent who services your machines.[2] None can get the parts we need for repairs.

We hope you can offer us a machine which gives better service. Will you[3] let us know what you plan to do? Sincerely yours, (69)

6

Dear Sir:

Now is the time to visit our shop. We have a new truckload of home furnishings which we are offering[1] at big, big savings to you.

Don't delay! Visit us now and choose from many fine items shown on each floor. Don't forget[2]—visit our shop now and save. Yours very truly, (50)

LESSON
6

WORD DEVELOPMENT

alCs *alC_* *alC-*

nvlv- *nvlvs* *nvlvm*

*pls_* *pls-* *rpls*

aplis *apli_* *apli-*

ascs *asc_* *asc-*

agre- *agre_* *agrem*

WORD CONSTRUCTION

cA- *scyl-*

ncrs- *sn-*

rc- *bs-*

su- *nf--*

frns- *alo-*

nsr- *am-*

READING AND WRITING EXERCISES

1

Dear David:

If you are willing to move back East and accept the job of plant manager, it will be necessary[1] for you to sign the enclosed agreement. After you return the agreement, we can determine when your duties[2] will begin.

I hope you will decide to be a member of our corporation. Sincerely, (57)

2

Dear Sir:

For a limited time, we will offer one week's free visit to our Cottages by the Sea. If you[1] accept, it will not be necessary for you to pay anything for your room and meals.

During your visit we will[2] show you new and used model cottages which you may buy on our easy payment plan, but don't delay. Why not call[3] now and determine a time for your free week?

We would like to show you how happy life can be at Cottages by[4] the Sea. Sincerely yours, (84)

3

Dear Sir:

We cash checks for residents of our town. After you have filled out the appropriate forms, you will receive[1] a check-cashing card which allows you to cash checks here at any time. We hope to serve you soon. Very truly yours,[2] (40)

4

Dear Ed:

Enclosed is a copy of the letter you wanted to see. The letter tells why it will be necessary[1] to increase our mailing fees and also how we determined the increases. After you have read the letter,[2] return it to the appropriate file. Sincerely, (49)

5

Dear Sir:

Having read your article on selling houses, I would like to ask you for a favor. Would you allow[1] us to reprint your article in our company bulletin?

We are certain what you say is true—the market[2] will get better when we see an increase in loan money. We are telling our agents to be patient, and your[3] article will help.

Will you let us know if we can use it? Respectfully yours, (74)

6

Dear Sir:

I would like to buy a copy of your new book, *How to Increase Retail Sales.* After reading a recent[1] review of the book, I believe it will help in a college course in which I have enrolled. Because classes have begun,[2] I need the book now. Could you rush a copy to my home address given in the above letterhead?

I have[3] attached a check to cover the price of the book and mailing fees. I will be eager to have your reply. Sincerely[4] yours, (81)

LESSON
7

**BRIEF
FORMS**

**BRIEF FORM
DEVELOPMENT**

rpl *fgln* *cn*
fgv *nf* *Ls*

ABBREVIATIONS

company	corporation	president
enclose, enclosure	and	vice president
information	return	east
west	north	south
Mr.	Mrs.	Miss
Ms.	catalog	

READING AND WRITING EXERCISES

1

Gentlemen:

We are happy you have decided to buy your new company cars from us.

Why don't you visit us[1] sometime during the week and determine which models you wish to buy? We have many cars which would be appropriate[2] for your corporation.

Our service people are very well trained and will keep your cars in top shape. At our firm,[3] we take pride in our service, and we want you to be happy. We are ready to help in any way we can.[4] Sincerely, (81)

2

Dear Sir:

Perhaps you have forgotten your payment is due. Would you take a minute to mail us a check?

We have been[1] patient, but we do not know if you have received our letters reminding you to make your payment on time. Won't you[2] call us? It is not necessary to pay your bill in full. If you cannot manage to pay the entire bill, we[3] will accept part of it.

If the current plan is too much for your budget, why not visit our loan office? Our agent[4] may be of help to you. Yours very truly, (89)

3

Dear Ed:

Enclosed is the information you wanted. It is a report based on an old market survey made by[1] our vice president. I hope you will forgive the delay in getting the information to you. We could not get[2] it by the time you wanted it because of our copy machine. The president of our firm sent the machine out[3] for repairs the same week we received your letter. We have a company policy which does not allow us to[4] take file items out of the office. Cordially yours, (89)

4

Dear Jill:

We are glad to report you have been accepted for classes beginning in the fall. We recommend you[1] plan now what courses you wish to take. The enclosed catalog should be of help.

You may be certain the skills you learn[2] here will be appropriate for any office. If you choose the medical or engineering fields, your training[3] will serve you well.

Do feel free to ask us for advice at any time. We are happy to be a part of your[4] future. Sincerely yours, (84)

5

Dear Richard:

Now is the time to plan our summer sale. Many retail managers hold large sales during different[1] times of the year. Why don't we try something new and determine a time for one big summer event? We can turn the[2] entire shopping center into a major sidewalk sale.

I would like to see the sale run for a full week. Perhaps[3] we could keep the shops open after regular closing times.

If you agree, I will talk to the merchants and let[4] you know what is decided. Yours truly, (87)

LESSON

8

WORD DEVELOPMENT

[shorthand outlines]

WORD CONSTRUCTION

[shorthand outlines]

WRITING ASSIGNMENT

[shorthand outlines]

4. *e cd fl . nu cl͡, e l ll u no f e rl . slm.*

5. *e r se . hu dm f r nu plse.*

READING AND WRITING EXERCISES

1

MEMO TO: Bob Smith

It is nearly time for our family camp to begin. We have not heard from all the families.[1] Will you call and remind them to fill out their health forms? The forms can be mailed to us. We really need the forms before[2] camp opens. (43)

2

MEMO TO: All Company Managers

Attached are the names of missing files. Apparently the files have been[1] misplaced. Would each of you look through your papers to see if the missing files could have been mislaid on your desk?

Many of[2] our folders are old and have misleading titles. Thus, mistakes can easily be made. (55)

3

Dear Mrs. Wilson:

I want to tell you how much I like the new health food displays you have in your pharmacy. It[1] is encouraging to see the growth in health foods in this city. I thought you would like to see the enclosed article[2] which discusses some reasons we are seeing such a rapid change in the health food market. Perhaps it will[3] encourage you to keep adding to your display. Sincerely, (70)

4

Dear Sir:

Recently I bought two lovely chairs from your company. Although the chairs have been used for a floor display,[1] neither showed any damage at the time. When the chairs arrived at my home, I felt very disturbed. To my dismay,[2] I discovered a rather large rip in the fabric. Either I did not see the rip when I bought the chairs, or it[3] happened during the trip to my house. In either case, the chairs will have to be returned. Sincerely, (77)

5

MEMO TO: All Marketing Heads

In your yearly report, will you discuss some new methods of marketing our new[1] engines? We are planning to set high goals for sales this year and need ways to help us achieve them. Perhaps you could give[2] us the results of your recent market research in which you asked dealers for their views on future sales. It may be[3] necessary to determine a new policy to be used in our company. If so, your report would[4] certainly be of help. (84)

LESSON

9

WORD DEVELOPMENT

aᴖls	aᴖl-	aᴖl̲
Nos	No-	No̲
lols	lol-	lol̲
neho	neʳ	nea
raplı	aplıs	aplı̲

WORD CONSTRUCTION

ar-	lor
hr	parl
hır	grr
hıl	lor̲
lruol	flogrf

WRITING ASSIGNMENT

1. e rcm uz̲ r nu Ccs.   l u ʌ h ⸴

3. u l v l pa ⸳
2. e l prN nu Ccs   mm fe + ᴖc ⸳
ʄ u ⸴ du u N   dpzl ʄ u N
s l ᴖl ⸳ Ccs   l uz r nu Ccs ⸴

4. *(shorthand outline)* ⌐ P Ns . cpe sN l eC v ⌐ brd mbrs .

5. *(shorthand outline)* ⌐ dsc clrc l rel ⌐ dpzl l u .

READING AND WRITING EXERCISES

1

MEMO TO: All Claims Managers

As head of this corporation, I was very happy to learn what a great job[1] you are all doing. A number of people have written to say that their claims were given very fine attention.[2] Without a doubt, all of you deserve credit for your part in giving this company a great name. (57)

2

Dear Sir:

Paying bills can mean headache after headache. That is why we are offering a new credit plan. With this[1] plan, you pay one total amount. Then we use that amount to pay all of the bills you owe.

If your bills are taking[2] too much cash from your budget, let us arrange an easy plan for you. Within a year, your bills will be paid and your[3] headache will be gone. Sincerely yours, (66)

3

Gentlemen:

We received your letter informing us that our seaside cottage will be reassessed on the 14th.[1] The letter went on to say that the value of this house increased greatly— by 25 percent—when the[2] new highway was built.

We are sorry, but you have made a mistake. The highway which runs near our beach house is not new.[3] If anything, it is old and badly in need of repair. The highway was built a few years after we bought our[4] beach house. To our knowledge, the road was never repaired after it was built.

We hope that your office will take a better[5] look at that highway. If our house is reassessed, we would like to see appropriate repairs made on the road.[6] Very truly yours, (124)

4

Dear Mr. Miller:

We did check to see if you will receive your cars on schedule. We called the trucking firm to[1] determine when the cars would arrive in New Haven, and the manager said the cars left early this morning. Although[2] some of the trucks are being delayed, yours should arrive on time this week. The manager assured us you will get a[3] call if there is anything new to report. We are happy to have been of help. Very truly yours, (78)

5

Dear Lou:

I received a letter from the Brown and Ames trucking firm asking for a copy of our yearly agreement.[1] I have looked in all of the file cabinets, but I have not seen the agreement. Could it have been misplaced? There are[2] two files which should have a copy of the agreement. Each copy seems to be missing. I hope you can advise[3] me on how to get a copy. Yours truly, (68)

LESSON 10

WORD DEVELOPMENT

PCs̲	*PCs-*	*PCss*
Psds	*Psd̲*	*Psd-*
rᵖds	*Pds̲*	*Pdss*
Pfls	*Pfl-*	*Pfl̲*
Pgrs-	*Pgrs̲*	*Pgrsv*

WORD CONSTRUCTION

Pgs	*Psyr*
Ppr-	*Ulgs*
Ppss	*Pvd̲*
Psnll	*Pss*
Pbls	*Ppz-*

WRITING ASSIGNMENT

1. *e l a d u l r / lol v u ln , sn hsp z sn z e blo . c ar / .*

2. *e r ncrs̲ r a d v u cr . r nu*

3. *e r ofr ls Cr / 20% ls ln r rglr prs .*

4. *dd u no la · gr No v lnaj drvrs r nsr-⌣ r fr.*

5. *n jn r lrn cls Nl evn lo lr₃ · gr dl v Dagrem.*

READING AND WRITING EXERCISES

1

MEMO TO: Manager of Purchasing

What is our current policy on purchasing office supplies? Which[1] companies have allowed us credit? Do we need a credit card to make a purchase, or can we provide our office[2] number?

Also, what is the name of the person who assigns credit cards? I hope you can provide me with this[3] information. It will be a great help to learn the proper purchasing methods. (74)

2

MEMO TO: All Personnel

Enclosed is a copy of the new proposal. As you can see, it provides many[1] needed changes. With this plan, each person will receive death benefits without paying for the increased coverage.[2] Personally, I believe this plan is what we have needed for many years. I see no problems with it at all.[3]

We are also revising our policy for training new personnel. Susan Jones is preparing a memo[4] which will provide all the details. I believe that these new policies will solve many problems in the company.[5] (100)

3

MEMO TO: Mr. Robert Temple

In my proposal for the new hospital, I plan to provide a design[1] for the building as well as general information needed to get a building permit. Why don't you prepare[2] a news release giving details of the proposal? Residents of this city should know that our hospital will[3] offer many new programs which will benefit out-patients as well as in-patients.

We have received much attention[4] from the newspaper recently due to increased hospital fees. This would seem to be an appropriate time[5] to let people know our plans to increase services. (109)

4

MEMO TO: James Brown

What is your advice on the attached health care program? With this program, the company would[1] provide a place, as well as a time, for running or swimming. It was proposed that we use the south side of the building[2] for this purpose. This plan was proposed by the president, who believes that people should be allowed to get proper[3] health care while on their jobs. Do you see any problems with such an arrangement? (74)

5

Gentlemen:

The purpose of this letter is to determine why we have not received the cards we purchased from your[1] company. When we decided to buy the cards, you were certain that we would have them ahead of time. As I[2] recall, we asked that the cards be rushed. Your agent assured us that there would be no problem during this time of the[3] year. We have been patient, but three weeks have gone by and we have not received the cards.

We hope that it will not be[4] necessary to cancel, but after this week we will not accept the cards. From now on, it would be appropriate[5] for you to inform us of delays by telegram. Yours truly, (110)

LESSON
11

WORD DEVELOPMENT

apy	*py-*	*pys*
avyds	*avyd-*	*avyd̲*
res	*Dre*	*re̲*
jyn-	*jyns*	*jyn̲*
mbrs	*mbrs*	*mbrss*

WORD CONSTRUCTION

syl	*suq-*
nyy-	*Ams*
nyz	*jyN*
yl	*rf-*
jy	*rsp̲*

WRITING ASSIGNMENT

1. ⌐ lol a ⌐l з du b ⌐ 12l, u all l ls ⌐lr d b · gr hlp.

lol No v ppl o ⌐ parl,

2. lr ⌐ з me m з lr ⌐ ⌐ m n ⌐

3. u l rsv u nu cr crd ⌐ol dla,

4. *[shorthand]*

5. *[shorthand]*

READING AND WRITING EXERCISES

1

Gentlemen:

In your letter of April 13, you referred to a delay in our January shipment of[1] office supplies. We are sorry for any problems caused by the delay, but our copy of the invoice shows that[2] your supplies were shipped as soon as payment was received. May we suggest this method for getting your shipment of[3] envelopes on time? You can avoid delay by mailing your check by May 30. Your envelopes will be shipped on[4] June 7 or the following week.

If you follow this plan for future purchases, we can provide you with better[5] service. Sincerely yours, (104)

2

Dear Jason:

Your recent appointment as vice president was great news. The company certainly made a wise choice.[1] As head of the shipping department, you provided many years of loyal service. It is reassuring to[2] see the company respond by giving you proper credit.

With your leadership, all departments will now operate[3] efficiently. I hope you will call on me to help in any way I can. As soon as you have some free time,[4] why

don't we get together for lunch? Very truly yours, (90)

3

Dear Sir:

Did you know that you may be paying between 15 and 20 percent too much for your insurance? Did[1] you also know that those policies may not cover the current value of your home and personal property?[2]

Now is the time to make certain that your benefits are all that you should have. Between March 15 and April 1,[3] our agent will call on you. Why not make it a point to have your policies ready for review? Cordially yours,[4] (80)

4

MEMO TO: Vice President Fowler

In regard to your memo of September 5, the printing machines will be[1] situated in our plant by the beginning of December. As you know, we wanted to have them ready[2] early in October but could not arrange to have them shipped at that time. We have asked a total of 30 machine[3] operators to participate in a training program during November, but we have not received responses[4] from all of them.

Perhaps we should plan to hire new people to operate the machines. What do you suggest?[5] (100)

5

MEMO TO: Fred Gray

I can now give you our new policy for insuring machines shipped by truck. Will you inform[1] all participating dealers that beginning July 1 we will not replace machines damaged on the dealer's[2] property? If the dealers wish to discuss this matter, refer them to the claims department.

We ask that any[3] damage be shown on the invoice at the point of arrival.

We would like the dealers to be told of the changes[4] now. Within a few weeks, letters will be mailed giving full details of the new policy. (96)

LESSON

12

WORD DEVELOPMENT

das   da   da-

dplca   dplca-   dplcas

⌒es   ⌒e   ⌒e

spras   spra-   spra

lca   lca-   lcas

WORD CONSTRUCTION

fra   si

Ae   uni-

ri   lrem

li   rla-

rgla   elma

WRITING ASSIGNMENT

1. Alo e v no jbs opn, ls ⌒ e Avz u l rapli ⌒ n r nu hsp opns. e l ⌒ arms l Dcs u L, la ⌒.

2. e l A. lol v 20 nu m l r parl. e l nd la me l hlp bld r nu hi a.

3. z. rls r co dz n

[Shorthand outlines]

4.

5.

READING AND WRITING EXERCISES

1

Dear David:

I was delighted to hear that you were promoted to department manager. Fred certainly chose[1] the right person for the job.

Now that you are part of the management team, I will enjoy seeing you regularly[2] at meetings. I know that this will be a busy year for you. If you have problems locating information,[3] I hope you will call on me. We all operate as a team here. Don't hesitate to ask for help. Cordially yours,[4] (80)

2

Gentlemen:

I have a problem. A shipment of white paint is due at my local dealer's by February 15.[1] I want very much to get this paint and begin decorating my new offices.

Your letter tells me that[2] a receipt for the paint was enclosed. The receipt was not in the letter. What shall I do?

Will I need the receipt[3] when I get the paint? If so, will you mail me a copy right away?

Call me if there is anything I need to[4] do. Yours very truly, (84)

3

Dear Editor Burns:

We were delighted with the great coverage you gave our fall carnival. We could not have hoped[1] for a better response than we received.

We are now inviting you to participate in an event we have[2] been planning for two years. This event will be called the Village Boat Show. The boats will be displayed in our village shopping[3] center. Right now it looks as though we may have some rather large boats here. If necessary, those boats will be located[4] in the east parking lot.

We are planning to have between 20 and 30 boats on display for one week[5] in April.

Will you plan to write an article to run during the week of the show? We also suggest running[6] an article sometime late in March. I feel certain that I could arrange a preview of the boats if that would help.[7]

Why don't we meet for lunch to discuss ways of promoting the show? Sincerely, (154)

4

Dear Sir:

Enclosed is your June billing. If you pay the total amount by the date shown on the bill, you will save money.[1] Following that date, a 5 percent fee will be added to your bill.

It would be wise to avoid late payments.[2] If your due date is a problem, you might wish to discuss new billing dates with our credit manager. If you call[3] for an appointment, the manager will be happy to plan a meeting time. Sincerely, (76)

5

MEMO TO: Vice President Roberts

We were all surprised to learn that President White resigned his office after[1] the board meeting. As you know, his proposal was defeated by a vote of 8 to 4. Evidently, the board's[2] vote was a deep personal disappointment.

We all feel sorry that the president felt it necessary to[3] resign. Much of this company's growth was related to his leadership. We hope the president will decide to[4] remain with this corporation. It might help if you would write a letter asking President White to meet with the[5] board this week. Perhaps it is not too late to change his mind on this matter. (113)

LESSON
13

WORD DEVELOPMENT

bqs	bq-	bq_
lqs	lq-	lq_
lqls	lqln	lqln_
alz-	alz_	alzs
alspas	alspa-	alspa_

WORD CONSTRUCTION

lq_	lqs
aq	drl
asr_	Gs
u'r	aqss
e'l	q-

WRITING ASSIGNMENT

1. r nu ofss l b sil- o r prp bln r ~m plM + r old ofs bld.

uz loz ~cs l sil frn= n r nu bld. a v r ppl l pp n r ~v.

2. r plM l n op bln Ja 28 + Fb 15, e l

3. du loz ~cs e suq la A sms

[Shorthand exercises]

4.

5.

READING AND WRITING EXERCISES

1

Dear Mr. Smith:

We are having a great number of problems with our Magic Teller bank machines. Evidently[1] they were not programmed to accept charge cards from this city. Will we have to replace the machines? We are hoping that[2] you can help us avoid doing that. New machines sell for a high price, while our used machines are worth little more than junk.[3]

Our marketing manager is planning to be in San Francisco very soon. Could you meet with him? Cordially[4] yours, (81)

2

Dear Miss Anderson:

Thank you for your letter regarding jobs for high school seniors. Your grades do indeed rank you at[1] the top of your class. We would be glad to have you apply. I am enclosing a company bulletin which will[2] supply many of the answers you need.

Although generally we need secretaries on a full-time basis,[3] we sometimes have a few part-time openings for high school juniors and seniors.

Bill Gray is a senior who is[4] finishing his second year with our firm. I suggest that you talk with him. You can also get more information from[5] our personnel manager, Mark Lee. If you cannot see him personally, his secretary will give you the[6] appropriate forms to fill out. Very truly yours, (129)

3

Dear Ms. Miller:

I am returning the blank check you sent us by mistake. We hope that you will mail us a second[1] check without delay. Because you have a good credit rating, you will not be charged a late fee.

We would like to[2] suggest that you use our printed envelopes for mailing your payments. Those envelopes are addressed to the credit[3] department, and your payments will be sent directly to the proper office.

Thank you for giving this matter your[4] attention. Yours truly, (84)

4

Dear Bob:

Thank you for your advice on the Frank Nelson case. Frank will be glad to know that a senior member of the[1] firm is willing to go to bat for him. Frank and I have had enough time to discuss his problem at length. Although[2] he does not anticipate receiving his old rank, Frank believes that a great number of people will benefit[3] if he wins this case. I think he is right, and we're hoping the judge thinks so too.

I'll certainly let you know if you[4] can help. Cordially yours, (84)

5

Dear Dr. Ames:

I want you to know that I am looking for more antique furnishings for your office. I have[1] located a desk and chair which I think you will like, but I am afraid that the length of the desk is not right for your[2] office. What would be a good time for you to look at it?

I also know of a nice antique desk for your[3] secretary. You'll love the light oak finish. I think it would be more appropriate for your waiting room than for your[4] office. We might have one problem. The shop manager is charging a great deal more than you may wish to pay. Perhaps we[5] can get him to take less. Let me know when I can show you these fine antiques. Sincerely yours, (116)

LESSON 14

BRIEF FORMS

la	ar	⌣
pp	bln	A
rsp	gr	3
3	⌣	hsp
loz	sil	jn
rf	prp	op
rsp	sug	⌢ dr
⌢	dr	h
G	q	ly
q	h	
h	py	

BRIEF FORM DERIVATIVES

arm	jnl	oprs
⌣n	⌣ol	zn
grl	rf-	A

ABBREVIATIONS

credit	number	insurance
regard	attention	amount
percent	envelope	department
invoice	total	junior
senior	second, secretary	

READING AND WRITING EXERCISES

1

Dear Mr. Brown:

It delights me to inform you that our credit department agreed to the total amount of[1] your loan. We can also arrange for a down payment of between 12 and 15 percent.

Your loan was referred to[2] the credit manager, and it received close attention. As you may know, we are having problems getting property[3] loans through. It was a help that your property is located near the new hospital. That adds a great deal to[4] the value of your property.

Would you return the enclosed agreement in the envelope provided? We will[5] need your response by February 10. Sincerely yours, (110)

2

MEMO TO: All Personnel

Here is great news for those of you who liked our old health plan. You will love our new one.[1]

Beginning August 15, we will offer a new policy which will provide many of the benefits you have[2] been asking for. It will pay as much as 80 percent of the total hospital bill. It also pays medical[3] fees and provides dental coverage as well.

With this plan, you can arrange for the insurance company to[4] pay your medical bills for you. There will be no need for you to write a check of your own. This service will save time[5] and money for you.

Those of you wishing to learn the details of this plan will be invited to discuss it in[6] a meeting at our office. (124)

3

Dear Susan:

We will soon be operating with new leadership. Recently the board voted to appoint a new[1] president. A number of names were suggested. An offer was made right away, but the person chosen did not[2] accept.

At this time I can say that we invited a very fine person to accept our offer, and she[3] responded well to it. Her name will be given at the board meeting on October 4. We hope that all board[4] members will be there to participate. Will you make arrangements for someone to be there from each of our departments?[5] Yours truly, (102)

4

Dear Mr. Evans:

This is in response to your letter telling us why we did not receive the January[1] shipment. I have discussed the problem with my people and can now tell you what happened.

We did have someone on duty[2] at the time the shipment arrived, but the shipment was not brought to the right place.

In the future, would you inform[3] your trucking firm that all shipments should arrive at the receiving dock on the east side of our building? We will be[4] certain to have a person there at all times to sign the invoice and accept the shipment. Very truly yours,[5] (100)

5

Dear Bill:

I had a good meeting with Dr. James. He

thinks we should purchase the model S80 unit. It[1] provides a direct link between the operator and the central memory bank. This is a new program which can[2] be offered at a minimum charge.

Dr. James feels that a second unit would allow us to operate even[3] more efficiently. I'll be glad to have your advice.

Do you anticipate going to the meetings in Las[4] Vegas? I will be there if I can get a direct flight from Denver. Very truly yours, (96)

LESSON

15

WORD DEVELOPMENT

Svz   Svzs   Svz-

dSs   dS_   dS-

mSs   mS_   mS-

elcl   elcll

elns   elnc

WORD CONSTRUCTION

Sbl   p

mS   'p

PS_   S rs

Ssd   Svzre

a Ss   elncs

WRITING ASSIGNMENT

1. nsr_ lnay drvrs c b . gr hdac. ndd s prMs v cl- hu a rbre. uf ur pa_ l C l nsr u lnay drvrs ll jn lf.

hlp. jn lf c nsr u lnayf 10% ls ln ne lry co n lon.

2. hr , gr nz f hd v f l. r hll bnfls no pa z C

[shorthand exercises]

READING AND WRITING EXERCISES

1

Dear Mrs. Brown:

Are you looking for a new electronic typewriter? We have a new model we call the[1] SUPERSONIC. It is a new type of electronic memory typewriter which will change your office routine.[2] This great little machine does big jobs. You name it. Our machine does it.

You and your secretary can operate it[3] easily. How? By pressing a few keys, you can produce a letter in seconds or an entire report in minutes.[4] You are the supervisor. The machine does all the hard jobs. Describing this unit as merely an electronic[5] typewriter would be a mistake. It is far more than that.

To show you what we mean, we are enclosing a brochure[6] describing how our machine operates. We are proud to say that the brochure was produced on this electronic[7] unit.

Let us show you more. Pay us a visit and try the SUPERSONIC. We think you'll love it. Sincerely,[8] (160)

2

Dear Fred:

I am delighted that your chain of super-markets will be joining our corporation. I hope it is[1] evident how happy we are to have you on board. You are now part of the family. We hope to see you[2] often.

In your letter accepting our offer, you used many generous words to describe my role. I am very[3] glad to have played a part in these happenings.

As a team, we are certain to achieve many changes in this firm.[4] It's good to know that you will be supervising the chain. Yours very truly, (94)

3

Dear Dr. Evans:

Dr. Green advised me that he will not be teaching for us this fall. As you know, Dr. Green[1] is an electrical engineer and head of the engineering department here. He is leaving our school to[2] join a local firm. As vice president, he will supervise electronic programming for the entire corporation.[3]

We are happy for Dr. Green, but sorry to see him go. He will not be easy to replace, but[4] corporations can pay electrical engineers more than we can.

Dr. Green is offering to write an ad[5] describing his job. I suggest that we place it in the engineering journals and see what happens. Yours truly,[6] (120)

4

Dear David:

I am afraid I will have to be away from the office for a week or so. During my trip out[1] West, I injured my back in a bad fall. The doctor prescribed medicine and a week in bed. I am hoping that[2] his advice will solve the problem. If it does not, the doctor may have to operate. It would then be necessary[3] for me to take a medical leave of three to four weeks.

I will let you know more as soon as I can. In the[4] meantime, I plan to keep writing at home. I am nearly finished with the report and feel certain that I can[5] supervise the research by phone as easily as I could in the office. Sincerely, (116)

5

Dear Evelyn:

What information do you have on electronic games? We are thinking of adding two new[1] models to our catalog. MR. AND MRS. SUPERMAN is a game appropriate for people between the[2] ages of seven and fifteen. We are also looking at a model called SUPERSONIC SPACESHIP. The point of this[3] game is to prevent a war between two superpowers. People of all ages like this game.

The market for[4] electronic games is changing rapidly. How are we to know which games to offer? We really need the benefit[5] of your knowledge. Won't you respond as soon as you can? Cordially yours, (112)

LESSON ▰▰▰▰▰▰▰▰▰▰▰▰▰▰
16

WORD DEVELOPMENT

p̲	p-	ps
aws	aw-	aw̲
rws	rw̲	rw-
grls	grls	grlh
bys	bys	byh

WORD CONSTRUCTION

pw	olw
nw	acw
fw̲	sdw
hrs	lvlh
hrl	brlrh

WRITING ASSIGNMENT

1. ⌐ dr gv h . q rpl + sm h h⌐ .

2. h ⌐ Ns lq a ̲a f . srl h⌐ .

3. e h . dla n ⌐ dr flu f⌐ dnvz l sn frnssco .

4. ⟋⌐ pln l G⌒
ln h Gs.

5. h, no sr VP
r bg.

READING AND WRITING EXERCISES

1

Dear Mr. Jones:

Our senior class was pleased to learn that you lived in our town during your childhood. As an executive[1] in a large corporation, you are a good example of someone from our own neighborhood who moved up to[2] the top of his field. We have voted you an award and are inviting you to be present at our awards night[3] on March 1.

During the program, we will present a look at the future, and we would appreciate having your[4] views on office careers. For example, what are some specific skills that executives and secretaries need?[5] We have heard that many companies are hiring now. What is the likelihood that we will get good jobs?

Any advice[6] you would like to give us will help us plan our futures. I will make copies of your response and distribute them[7] to the entire class. Very truly yours, (148)

2

Dear Howard:

Your letter brought back pleasant boyhood memories from the days when I was growing up on College[1] Avenue. Tell your class I would be pleased to accept their award in person. Let me know what hours you would like me to[2] be present.

It is rewarding to know that you are looking ahead. There are many issues facing executives[3] today, but the chief problem is locating good people to keep the office running efficiently.

Any[4] good executive relies upon the help of a skilled secretary. Secretaries need a wide range of skills,[5] from managing company records to producing correspondence that is free of errors. He or she also[6] needs to be a person who relates well to all types of people.

I look forward to meeting you and discussing[7] these issues in greater detail. Sincerely yours, (149)

3

Dear Mrs. Green:

Thank you for your letter informing us that your mailing address will be changing soon. We will make[1] the change in our records as soon as we receive the enclosed form. Please give us specific information for[2] forwarding your correspondence. Print or type your house number and the full name of your avenue or boulevard. Be[3] certain to specify the month and day you wish to begin receiving mail at your new address.

We suggest that[4] you mail notices to people you correspond with on a regular basis. We would be happy to supply[5] you with the appropriate forms. Cordially yours, (109)

4

Dear Members:

The topic of this month's meeting will be "Girlhood Dreams." The meeting will be held in the old school[1] building on North Shore Boulevard. Perhaps we can all share childhood memories while we are there.

Please notice that our[2] meeting is being moved up to a new hour. It was also suggested that we change our regular meeting day.[3] Please be prepared to discuss whether we should move it up toward the beginning of the month.

I will distribute[4] copies of our recent survey in which we asked you to specify goals for the new year. Your answers were very[5] rewarding, and I look forward to sharing them with you. I hope you will all be present. Very truly yours,[6] (120)

5

Dear Henry:

Thank you for forwarding a set of your designs for the new electric engine. Now that we have had[1] some time to look at them, we are delighted to say that we think you have given us a fine example for the[2] future, as well as the present.

We have decided to distribute copies to our field engineers, and we have[3] asked them to respond in 30 days. In all likelihood we will hear from them even before then. I am sure[4] you will be as eager as I am to see their reports, so I will forward them as soon as I can.

We appreciate[5] the efficient service you have given us. Sincerely yours, (111)

LESSON 17

WORD DEVELOPMENT

WORD CONSTRUCTION

WRITING ASSIGNMENT

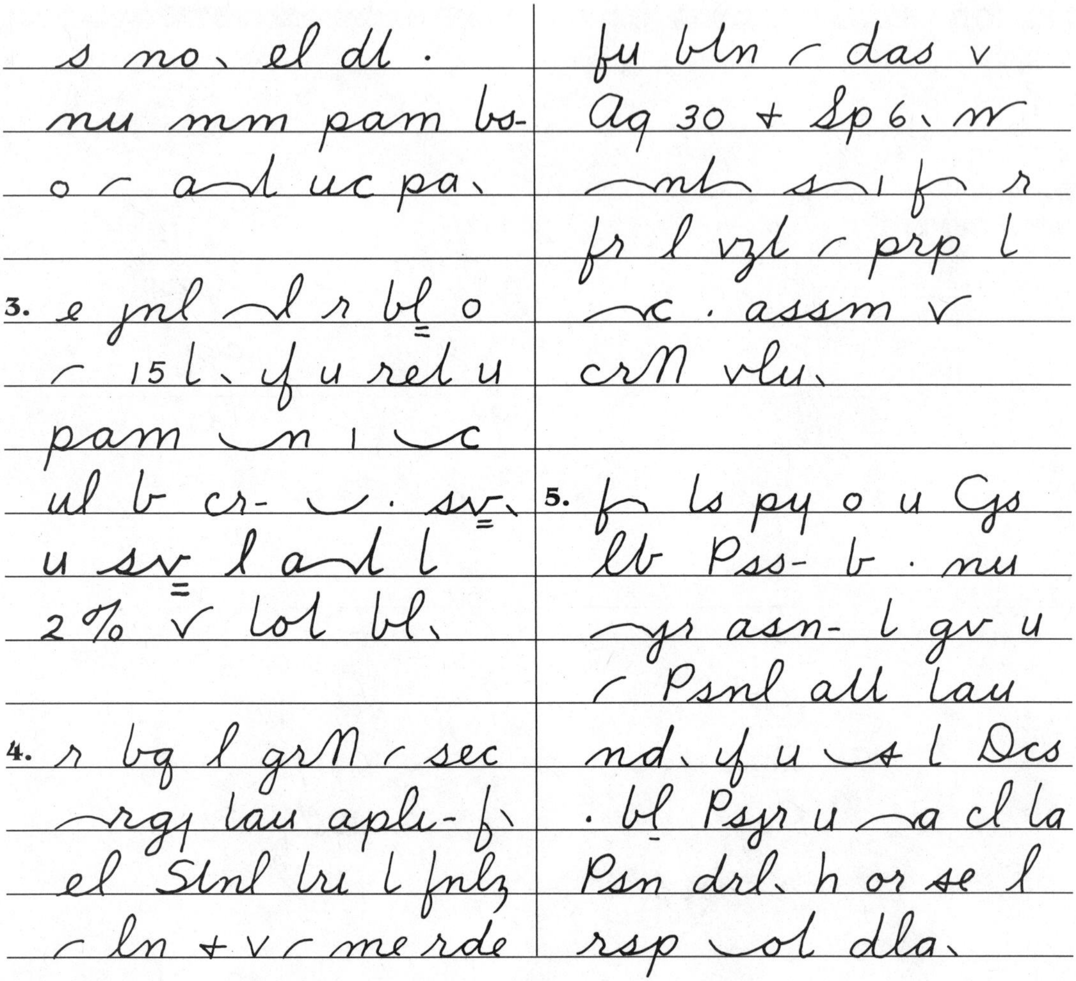

READING AND WRITING EXERCISES

1

MEMO TO: Members of the Board

I am recommending Dr. Albert Brown for a position on our Board of[1] Directors. Dr. Brown was a physician here for more than 20 years. Some of you may remember the firm[2] leadership he provided for our neighborhood schools. For example, it was Dr. Brown who urged a decision in[3] favor of building South Junior High. He also raised revenue to purchase the property for an addition[4] to that building.

I believe Dr. Brown will agree to head our drive for better educational programs. He[5] takes charge of tough situations and is not afraid to go on record for what he thinks is right. This man ranks highly[6] as a leader in our city. (126)

2

Dear Ms. Smith:

Thank you for your letter of application. At the present time we have no openings in the[1] department of fashion design. I am forwarding your letter to our marketing division with the suggestion[2] that the manager correspond directly with you.

We are producing a new fashion line which will be ready[3] for distribution between July 15 and July 30. We may decide to market these items on a[4] national basis. If so, it will be necessary to add more personnel. Your education and training[5] would seem to be appropriate for such a position.

If you do not hear from the manager within a few[6] days, perhaps you should give him a call. In the meantime, I will be happy to keep a copy of your letter[7] in our records. If our situation does change, we will let you know. Cordially yours, (155)

3

Dear Mr. and Mrs. Gray:

Remember when the two of you hoped to enjoy the vacation of your dreams aboard[1] an ocean liner? Year after year you wanted to go, but didn't. Could the problem have been money?

If your[2] answer is yes, we have a solution for you. Our ship will sail on the morning of May 10 to seven different[3] ports on the Atlantic Ocean. What a vacation that will be! If you have had a relationship with our bank[4] for three years or more, you will receive a reduced rate. In addition, senior citizens may participate in[5] a credit plan with low monthly payments.

We can accept applications no later than April 1, so please don't[6] delay. It's a boat you can't afford to miss. Cordially yours, (131)

4

Dear Shelley:

The news from our nation's capital is not good these days. It appears that neither the House nor the[1] Senate will accept the President's budget during this session. Because of the delays here, I will be returning[2] to my office a few days later than I had planned. Will you please answer all correspondence while I am away?[3]

I don't have a solution to the budget issue. It's a tough problem. I will let you know as soon as I hear[4] something further. In the meantime, please refer all calls directly to our press secretary.

Do you know where to[5] locate specific information on the local labor situation for me? I would appreciate your[6] help. Yours truly, (123)

5

Dear Jim:

What do you think of the enclosed article written by Susan Williams? It shows how we could increase[1] out-patient services as a way of reducing hospital fees. Dr. Williams says that with proper supervision,[2] more patients could be released on the day after an operation. In many cases, the person could go[3] home on the same day.

I believe we should look into what Dr. Williams is saying. She is providing a great[4] service by giving us these suggestions. If you agree, I will distribute copies to all executives.[5] Perhaps we can use the article to determine new policies here. Yours very truly, (116)

LESSON 18

WORD DEVELOPMENT

_Oa_	_⌐o_	_Ol_
ins	_in_	_in-_
odl	_od_	_rod_
_ds_	_ld_	_hld_
_⌐ls_	_ℓ_	_ℓ-_

WORD CONSTRUCTION

rod	_hsn_
Odu	_Ulc_
Olc-	_Uri_
Ohd	_Uscr_
_Ol_	_Uln_

WRITING ASSIGNMENT

1. _idap ✓ if ud sp ⌐ ins u ✓ ɬ lse, ⌐ ⌐ns l sp dlrs n ls lon,_

2. _p ll ⌐e no if ucl P ⌐ ⌐e,_

3. _e pln l D loz_

4. _ll ⌐e no ⌐n ⌐ h , p,_

5. _hu l P ⌐ Pq f s ×_

READING AND WRITING EXERCISES

1

Dear Mrs. Smith:

There is truth in the saying, "You are what you eat." Think about the billions of meals that are[1] prepared yearly.

To be a great cook, you need cookbooks you can rely upon. Why not join our cookbook club for great[2] dining enjoyment? As a member of our cookbook club, you can learn to prepare great daily meals. You will also[3] save money at the supermarket. There is more good news—your membership fee is included in the purchase[4] of three or more books.

Enclosed is a brochure which describes a new cookbook we are offering. It has won five[5] national awards. Why not try it for two weeks with no obligation to buy? If you decide to keep your copy,[6] mail us a check or money order for $15.95. This book would make a great gift for the[7] holidays.

Please use the enclosed form to specify the number of copies you wish to order. You may charge your[8] purchases, or we will bill you directly. We can accept cancellations up to ten days following the date[9] your order is received. Yours very truly, (188)

2

Dear Mr. May:

As you know, we have had some problems with the word processing unit we purchased from your firm.[1] Overall, the machine operates well, but it does not do all of the tasks we believed it would do. Your agent has[2] recommended that we increase the central memory bank by adding features to it. We feel that the added[3] features should have been included under the terms of our original agreement. Will we be charged the full[4] amount for the changes we are forced to make?

We need a decision soon and look forward to your advice on this[5] matter. Sincerely yours, (104)

3

Dear Mrs. Parker:

Join us and use our new checking service. It's very easy.

What does our bank offer you? We[1] have many checking plans to meet your needs. For example, if you keep a minimum of $200 in[2] the bank, there will be no service charge. If you don't wish to keep a minimum amount, you can pay a monthly fee[3] of $4.50. You may prefer to pay for each check you write at 10¢ per check.

There is no limit[4] on the number of checks you may write. If you order now, you will receive 200 checks free of charge. Drop by[5] your local branch office on Shoreline Avenue and let us tell you more about our checking and savings plans. Our[6] banking services are designed to make efficient money management easy for our customers. Cordially[7] yours, (141)

4

Dear Members of the Board:

Attached is a copy of our new operating budget. As you can see, the total[1] amount is a little under $2,000,000. This is an increase of nearly $225,000[2] over the old budget. Part of the increase is due to our plans to purchase property for two proposed[3] plants. Even with the property purchases, the budget seems too high.

Therefore, I am appointing a group of[4] executives to review these figures and recommend specific cuts. I hope that some of you will participate[5] in that review. I would also appreciate hearing your suggestions at the board meeting on June 2. Please[6] plan to be present on that day. Sincerely yours, (129)

5

Dear Mrs. Carlson:

We regret to inform you that the blue fabric you ordered is not made in a 54-inch[1] width. Could you use it in a 45-inch width? Although we do not currently have the 45-inch fabric[2] in our shop, we would be happy to order it for you. Such orders take about two to three weeks to arrive.[3]

The remaining items you specified were shipped today. The total amount of your order is[4] $79.96. Of course, that amount does not include the price of the blue fabric or its shipping[5] charges. The shipping weight of the 45-inch fabric is 7 pounds 6 ounces.

We look forward to serving[6] you in the future. Yours truly, (125)

LESSON
19

WORD DEVELOPMENT

eqll   *eqls*   *eql_*
eqp-   *eqps*   *eqpm*
alrz-   *alrzs*   *alrz_*
las   *lar*   *lars*
aqMs   *aqM-*   *aqM_*

WORD CONSTRUCTION

*adl_*   *qcr*
al-lc   *adlr*
alrs   *alrz*
ql   *qo-*
Aqll   *frqMl*

WRITING ASSIGNMENT

1. *p gr ~e c m*   *hr la h or se arvs*
   vr ave or blvd   *eC d.*
   f r recs.

3. *~r sno , . ex*
   ~ r fr.

2. *du ls ~o er asc_*
   eC Psn l rec c

4. *il so u . ex ✓ cos er lc f .*

5. *ho ofn du u cos ᴜ h .*

READING AND WRITING EXERCISES

1

Dear Mr. Wilson:

Our office building is quite old. Recently we were told that our lighting is not adequate[1] to meet current laws. We are faced with a decision. Can we solve the problem by equipping all desks with electric[2] lamps, or should we call in a company such as yours to replace our overhead lights with new units?

Our[3] electrical engineer has said that new overhead lights would provide better lighting. He also added that the[4] total amount for such a purchase could run about $2,000 or more. We are hesitant to allow[5] the price to go over $2,000 because many of our people have suggested that they would be[6] equally happy with electric lamps.

Would you be willing to give us your suggestions on how to solve our problems?[7] I would appreciate your response as quickly as you can give it to us. Cordially yours, (156)

2

Dear Customer:

Could your family use a second car? If so, we have the auto for you. This model is great[1] for frequent trips about town, but it's equally good for highway driving. Either way you plan to use it, this auto[2] will save money on gasoline. It gets better mileage than any new model currently on the market.[3]

During the month of February, we are authorized to sell this car at a very low price. Believe it or[4] not, that price will include your choice of equipment. Won't you drive by our showroom and see this great value?

While you're here,[5] sign up for our free drawing. A lovely new car will be awarded to a lucky resident of our city.[6] That winner could be you. Yours truly, (126)

3

Dear Ms. Lee:

Thank you for your letter regarding a position with our firm. Enclosed is a brochure describing[1] our policy on the education you will need. As you can see, we generally ask that all management[2] trainees have a college degree. In a few cases we have offered positions to people who have had some college-[3]level courses and related job skills, even if they did not have a degree.

For further information,[4] please call or write our personnel division located at 412 Elm Boulevard. We recommend that you mail[5] us a copy of your resumé accompanied by a letter of application. In your letter, be certain[6] to mention any additional skills or training you may have received outside college courses. Sincerely[7] yours, (141)

4

Gentlemen:

Thank you for your letter of May 12. You were quite right. The total amount of the bill should have been based[1] on the quote we gave you a few months ago. We are making the change in our records, and your invoice will show the[2] new amount.

You were charged full price because we had not informed our agent of the agreement we had made with you.[3] From now on, we will see to it that all parties are operating under the same agreement. We appreciate[4] your order and will have the equipment shipped to you by the date you specified.

I am glad you brought this matter[5] to my personal attention and look forward to serving you in the future. Yours very truly, (119)

5

Dear Meg:

We were quite surprised by the response to the opening of our new shop. Although we anticipated[1] having between 300 and 400 people, more than 600 customers were present for the event.[2]

The total amount of sales was well over $15,000. Our general manager feels that this large[3] turnout was the result of a super promotion effort. She has asked me to thank each member of the team. That[4] includes you.

You gave us many fine suggestions. In addition, you played a major role in overseeing the[5] event and by setting up the free drawings and awarding prizes.

Your efforts are appreciated. Yours truly,[6] (120)

LESSON 20

WORD DEVELOPMENT

alM-	*alMs*	*alM̲*
Nca̲	*Ncas*	*Nca-*
nlM-	*nlM̲*	*nlMs*
soM-	*soMs*	*soM̲*
rfMs	*rfM-*	*rfM̲*

WORD CONSTRUCTION

cM	*bhM*
dpM	*spM̲*
boM	*aroM̄*
hMs	*cMr*
frMs	*bcgroM*

WRITING ASSIGNMENT

1. ⌐ enc- cal Is
O 2H us lau
Ks ⌐a od drl
f r nɟl sls
ofs、

2. p rm Ks L ru
⌐ prs v eC
us U ⌐ apo
od No、

3. efl la · sec

[shorthand outlines]

rpl , n od
bf —c frls
plns f · S —r f
1M 2H T $,

4. u —a PCs —
20 = lb ppr f
60²⁴ +r prs

ds 4 Gs U ls
agrem ,

5. (mr +os lau
prs v 4230⁵⁴ ds
Gs f ne Am O
(—a v 2T lbs ,

READING AND WRITING EXERCISES

1

Dear Howard:

You will be pleased to hear that I am making progress on the profit and loss report you wanted. You[1] should have it by the time your group meets again.

I quite agree that we should make some changes in our management of[2] capital. To make those decisions, we should take a good look at the national economy. I have read[3] several articles suggesting that this is not an appropriate time to buy or sell bonds, so there would be little[4] advantage to cashing in our dividends now.

In general, I would also recommend against buying land[5] for two reasons—property values are high and mortgage money is hard to obtain. I believe we should look into[6] buying farm land. The Secretary of Agriculture has proposed legislation which would permit new farm[7] owners to get loans at a percentage rate well under the present market rate. Yours very truly, (158)

2

MEMO TO: Elizabeth Brown, Director of Purchasing

We are planning to send about 2,000 letters[1] for our fund drive. Included with each letter will be a return envelope. Would it be more economical[2] for us to use the window envelopes we are now using in our office? Perhaps we should order regular[3] business envelopes. I know that regular envelopes can be purchased for less money, but we would have to pay[4] charges for having our address added to each envelope.

If we decide to order envelopes, we should do[5] so right away to make certain that they can be shipped without delay. I am inclined to order more window[6] envelopes.

If it would save time for you, we would be happy to place our own order and have the invoice mailed directly[7] to the purchasing department. (146)

3

Dear Mary:

Enclosed is a copy of the invoice from Roadway Truck Lines saying that they have not been paid for the[1] handling charges on the recent shipment we received. I have checked the receipt and found that we paid a total of[2] $638.59—which is more than the amount of our regular shipments.

Can[3] you find out where the problem is? If the handling charges were not included in our regular payment, we paid[4] too much for the shipment. If they were included, we should send that information to the trucking lines.

A similar[5] situation occurred several months ago, and we found that the trucking firm had made a mistake. It would[6] be to our advantage to check the matter closely. Very truly yours, (133)

4

Dear Friend:

To show you how much we appreciate your business, we are planning a sales event. During the month of[1] April, we will mark 20 percent off all carpeting. As our credit card customer, you will be invited[2] to choose any kind of carpet you wish. For example, those regularly priced at $14.99[3] per square yard will be offered at $11.96 per square yard. What an economical way[4] to add new life to your home!

We hope you will take advantage of this great offer. We will be happy to pay you[5] a personal visit to determine the number of square yards you will need. This is our way of saying thank you[6] for your business. Sincerely yours, (126)

5

Dear Chris:

I received your copies of the new land leasing agreements. They appear to be in order, but we are[1] not yet certain whether or not we can get permission to drill. As you know, new legislation could prevent us[2] from drilling on certain kinds of agricultural land. It now looks as if those laws will not apply to companies[3] drilling less than 900 feet into the ground. It is not quite clear whether the law applies to natural[4] gas or if it is limited to oil wells.

Our president has written to Senator Brown to get more information,[5] but I am afraid we will not have a definite answer for several weeks. About all we can do[6] now is remain patient. Yours truly, (126)

LESSON

21

ABBREVIATIONS

avenue	pound	day
billion	inch	record
square	hundred	agriculture
month	boulevard	thousand
hour	ounce	feet
million	dollar, dollars	economic, economy
example, executive	cent, cents	yard

BRIEF FORMS

[shorthand outlines]

READING AND WRITING EXERCISES

1

Dear Mr. Wilson:

Enclosed is the bill for repairing your television set. As you can see, the charges total[1] $59.95. This price includes a 30-day guarantee on parts and service. If you[2] have more problems, be certain to call our customer service department while the repairs are under warranty.[3] We will visit your home and make the repairs at no additional charge to you.

Your set is in good shape generally[4] and should provide you with many years of good service, but why not think about adding a second set to your[5] home? We have several models which you could easily move from room to room. If you buy now, we will include[6] a fine rolling cart free of charge with your purchase. We hope you'll take advantage of our offer. Sincerely yours,[7] (140)

2

Dear Jason:

As I was preparing the program for our meeting, I discovered that we have several items[1] of new business to cover. Now I am afraid that our meeting will run over the time we have allowed. Can you[2] meet with me in order to go over some of these items? Perhaps some of them can be handled at a future[3] meeting.

Also, do you plan to present your findings on the marketing survey? If so, please let me know how much[4] time you will need. Our building manager has taken a position against purchasing certain kinds of electrical[5] equipment. He anticipates taking about ten minutes to discuss specific examples.

I have asked[6] each department manager to be present for this meeting. So far I have received one cancellation. Ms.[7] Wilson called to say that she will be on vacation that week and has asked Dr. Evans to take her place. Yours[8] truly, (161)

3

Gentlemen:

I am quite surprised that we have not heard from you regarding the marketing books we ordered.

When we[1] placed the order, we were assured that the books would be shipped directly from your plant by the day specified. When the[2] books did not arrive on time, my secretary called the supervisor of your shipping department. The supervisor[3] found that the order placed by our business education department had been overlooked. He promised to send[4] the shipment right away.

More than a week has gone by, and we have no books. We plan to distribute them during[5] the opening class session on August 19. Please let us know what you plan to do about this matter. We would[6] appreciate hearing from you very soon. Very truly yours, (131)

4

Dear Miss Collins:

This is in response to your letter of application. It so happens that we are looking for[1] a person to replace our correspondence secretary, who is being promoted to a different[2] position.

I am attaching a copy of the job description. If you wish to apply for this specific[3] position, please write a letter indicating when you would be free to begin and the level of salary you[4] desire. Please remember to include a copy of your resumé with the letter.

We hope to choose final[5] candidates within a few days, so we would like to have your letter no later than February 1. Yours very[6] truly, (121)

5

Dear Dr. Mason:

I enjoyed reading your manuscript on managing our natural environment. You[1] certainly offer a clear view of the problems facing our economy. I was quite pleased with your suggestions for[2] locating new reserves of oil, for example. Your solution seems to be one that no one else has thought of.

I[3] agree entirely with your views on outdated leasing agreements and free use of agricultural land.[4] It is quite clear that all parties would benefit from changing these laws.

I wish you well in finishing this book and will[5] gladly help if the need arises. Cordially yours, (109)

LESSON
22

WORD DEVELOPMENT

qls	qlr	qlrs

WORD CONSTRUCTION

WRITING ASSIGNMENT

1. wb alrz- l qo · nu prs fu ppr bs- o · od v 2T5H lbs.

la hsp + dNl Gs lb Aqll cvr- U ls nu bnfl pln.

2. e ⌣ v p- lse

3. ec Pss ods ⌒C

~ qcl no la
eno ho luz r
ab-a- eqpm.

4. ed v lpa · ~ol
Svo G v 79 $
f eqpm PCs-
U r bns v

ls agrem.

5. ucb Sln la
18 yds √ 54 = un
fbrc l Aqll
cvr r Crs uv
dS-.

READING AND WRITING EXERCISES

1

Dear Dr. Davidson:

Recently, I was a patient under the care of your efficient personnel. I[1] especially appreciated the efforts of your nurse, Ellen Jeffries. It is not easy to find people who[2] perform over and above the call of duty, but Ms. Jeffries is one of those rare persons. I was impressed by[3] her kind manner, her dedication, and the prompt attention she gave to every patient under her care.

She was[4] never too busy to listen to our problems and often did so on her own time. I believe her character[5] was encouraging to the other personnel as well as to the patients.

It was very satisfying to[6] see the high level of professional care throughout your hospital. I wanted you to know personally that[7] the other patients and I appreciated it. Sincerely yours, (152)

2

Gentlemen:

Thank you for your questions regarding our shipping and distribution policies. We offer several[1] plans. Many large businesses take advantage of the following budget plan.

If you order a minimum[2] of $12,000 in merchandise per year, you will receive a reduced rate which can be paid in one amount[3] yearly or four amounts quarterly. For every additional shipment, you will pay only 10 percent of your[4] regular shipping fee.

Another plan we suggest is an arrangement often used by small retail businesses.[5] You place orders as you need them and are billed for each order. If your total shipments for any given year[6] amount to more than $7,200, you will receive a savings which will be credited toward[7] your purchases the following year.

We will be happy to discuss other plans to meet your needs. Please feel free to[8] call on us at any time. Yours truly, (167)

3

Dear Sir:

I have several questions about your university. Would you please send me a copy of your[1] catalog, an application form, and other general information regarding enrollment policies? I[2] am enclosing copies of my academic records, which I hope you will find satisfactory. Are there other[3] courses I should take to ensure that my application will be accepted?

I would also like specific[4] details about your School of Business. Currently I am thinking of majoring in marketing, with an emphasis[5] in merchandising and marketing analysis. I hope you can advise me on other fields such as[6] personnel management, sales management, economics, etc.

I have been told that you place seniors in jobs[7] related to their chosen fields for one full quarter during the final year. Is this the case for every senior?[8] I would also appreciate receiving whatever information you have about job markets in business[9] and industry. Yours very truly, (186)

4

Dear Mr. and Mrs. Ames:

We want this holiday season to be especially happy for you and your[1] family. That's why we designed a holiday budget plan—to make your shopping easier and your holidays[2] happier.

Our budget plan provides the cash you need and an easy payment schedule. Here's how we can help you.[3] Visit our loan department and talk with our credit

officer. When you have determined the amount of cash you need,[4] you can choose a payment plan designed to fit your monthly budget. If you wish, you may delay making payments up[5] to 90 days following the loan.

You will find our service prompt and our officers eager to help. By serving[6] customers like you, we have learned how to make the holidays an easier time for many people, and we take[7] pride in doing so.

While you are here, ask for information on our full line of banking services. We think[8] you will be impressed with the wide range we offer. At General Savings and Loan, when we add a new customer,[9] we know we have made a new friend. Very truly yours, (189)

5

Dear Dr. Sharp:

Thank you for your correspondence asking about our plans for publishing your book, *Guide to Word[1] Processing*. I think I can now answer those questions to your satisfaction.

We anticipate having the books on[2] the market by the end of February or the beginning of March. I am very pleased to report that we[3] had the manuscript reviewed by several people in the industry and received very good responses. They[4] were especially impressed with the final chapter in which you discuss other uses for electronic[5] equipment in the office.

Because your manuscript is so timely, we wish to prepare it for future use as[6] quickly as we can. We believe your book is a very good example of what our readers want. I will make every[7] attempt to keep you up to date on what's happening. Yours very truly, (153)

LESSON
23

WORD DEVELOPMENT

aks	*ak_*	*akN*
ayš-	*ayš_*	*ayšm*
asš-	*asš_*	*asšN*
cšs	*cš_*	*cšl*
kdys	*kdy-*	*kdy_*

WORD CONSTRUCTION

kpur	*rgš*
Amšr	*bš*
Aņš	*kNs*
kšrcy	*šc*
kncy	*šdNs*

WRITING ASSIGNMENT

1. *ulb p- lno la* | *l Dcs ⌐ rl*
   er pln_ sv ⌐e | *la agr plas n*
   l lc ab crN | *r lcl + nyl*
   lrNs ⌐ eco. | *ecos×*

2. *lu alN ⌐ ⌐e*   3. *er enc_ · cpe*

vu od f 18 H
sq yds v crpl
lae Pss- ld.

4. *p Nca nr sps*
U r uns dSg
r No v bs crds
lau ⌣ + l od.

5. *ern Sln y 880*
sq yds v crpl
lb Agl l cvr
8T sq fl v flr
sps z sn n
u plns.

READING AND WRITING EXERCISES

1

Gentlemen:

It was most satisfying to read your article concerning air traffic. When the airport was built,[1] the runway size was more than adequate. During the last several years, conditions have greatly changed. We now have[2] a much larger number of aircraft using our airport on a daily basis.

I agree that the cost of[3] increased services should not be paid by the city alone. It would be more economical for everyone[4] if the county were to pay a greater share of the costs. Personally, I would like to see a proposal placed before[5] the county council asking for an increase in funding.

Do you know if anyone has investigated[6] using other revenue? I would be willing to help start a fund drive in order to raise money from private[7] sources such as business, industry, and foundations. Perhaps you could address this topic in a front-page story.[8]

The need for increased services is a major issue today. I hope you will keep giving it the coverage[9] it deserves. Sincerely yours, (185)

2

Dear Mr. and Mrs. Smith:

I was delighted to receive your call asking me to be your real estate agent.[1]

I believe that your asking price is right. You have a fine home in a very good location. There is every reason[2] to believe that your home will be sold in a very short time. As I mentioned earlier, your house will be listed[3] in the newspaper as well as in our real estate bulletin. The bulletin is published on a weekly[4] basis and distributed all over the county in stores and office buildings. It is well read and often gives[5] the best results of all sources used.

We will show your home as frequently as we can. To make those visits more pleasant[6] for you, I will call at least one hour ahead of time to make an appointment. The decision whether or not[7] to remain at home during those visits is entirely up to you.

I look forward to serving as your agent.[8] Very truly yours, (164)

3

Dear Ms. Miller:

We have sent several notices informing you that your account is past due, and still we have[1] not heard from you. Almost three months have gone by, and we have not received your check. Is there some reason you cannot send[2] even the minimum payment?

There is still time to make your account current and maintain your good credit standing.[3] Please call our office today and make arrangements to settle this matter.

We will be glad to help in any way.[4] If we understand your problem, perhaps we can arrange a payment schedule to accommodate your needs. Yours truly,[5] (100)

4

Dear Ms. Williams:

Professor Brown tells me that you have written several articles about the computer[1] industry. I have just finished a study on using computers in education, and I would like to share my[2] findings with you. The enclosed report is based on my research. Would you take a look at it and tell me if you think[3] the report could be published as a book?

Almost all of the report concerns new uses for computers in the[4] classroom. At present, I am testing the methods in my own classroom and making arrangements to have them tested[5] elsewhere. The responses from teachers have been very good.

I would like to present my report to a publisher[6] and would appreciate any suggestions you have about writing a detailed proposal. I hope you can find[7] time in your busy schedule to give me your comments. I would greatly value your advice and am prepared to pay[8] a fee for this service.

Please let me know if you can help. Cordially yours, (173)

5

Dear Lisa:

Thank you for your comments on our proposed shopping center. We are pleased to say we will present our plans[1] to the city planning commission on January 11.

I especially appreciate your[2] advice in regard to providing necessary information. The report you included with your letter[3] provided a fine example to follow. I believe our request for a zoning change will be granted. A[4] location west of town is the best choice for a large center like ours.

Our shopping center will contain several large[5] businesses—three discount stores, five department stores, and two supermarkets. It will accommodate up to[6] 100 other businesses.

The center should draw customers from several counties. Thus, it will increase commerce[7] for the entire city. For that reason, we anticipate a great deal of support for our plan. Yours very truly,[8] (160)

LESSON
24

WORD DEVELOPMENT

kus	ku-	kuy
lks	lk-	lk_
ak-	ak_	akm
kps	kp_	kpl
reps	rep-	rep_

WORD CONSTRUCTION

ʃS	lS_
kvny	Sde
Sam	kln-
krs	plSc
kn	USN_

WRITING ASSIGNMENT

1. edap v · P∧
   D v qr zlz
   ⌐ ol inf,

   U esp nr dpl
   v bʒ,

2. er atʌ l ∧e
   ncrs- nrlm nr

3. ιdlc l ∿fsʒ
   aq ho ∿c e
   nyy- lc_ · lʃ

vu n.   *g.*

4. *y udu n fn ls ~dse Ub 1H% sat u me lb ret- lu ~ot*

5. *s crc v E brnC ofs L Pvd P~t + frnl Svo L E K.*

READING AND WRITING EXERCISES

1

Gentlemen:

We have good news for you. Your shipment of office furnishings came in last Friday. Will it be okay[1] to deliver it this week?

If you have a specific day in mind, please call our shipping department and make the[2] arrangements directly with them. Otherwise, someone will be in touch with you. It would also be wise to confirm[3] your street address.

As soon as you accept delivery, please check each item with care. When you are satisfied that[4] the shipment is complete and contains no damaged goods, return one copy of the invoice with your full payment.

Thank[5] you for allowing Movers, Inc., to handle these shipping arrangements for you. Please call on us[6] again. We are a brief phone call away from serving you. Sincerely yours, (132)

2

Dear Frank:

A question came up Thursday concerning our lease agreement on the old federal building. This morning[1] a government representative called to ask if we still wish to purchase the property. A firm called Investors,[2] Inc., has made an offer and is waiting for a reply. What do you think about this opportunity?[3]

The building has about 10,000 square feet of floor space, and we are using about 60 percent of it.[4]

We have often discussed whether we should buy the building, continue renting, or move to a new location.[5] Now the time has come to make a decision about this capital investment. Very truly yours, (119)

3

MEMO TO: All Sales Personnel

You should be especially pleased with

your accomplishments this year. We not only[1] met our sales goals, we surpassed them.

This year's record sales offer a fine opportunity to point out the[2] contributions made by sales representatives. The growth of our corporation is directly related to your[3] outstanding efforts.

As we look ahead to the coming year, let's set our goals for continued growth in the marketplace.[4] I feel confident that the new year will yield the best results ever. When we meet again at the regional[5] convention, we will discuss how to achieve those results.

Please accept the enclosed bonus check with our compliments.[6] It is our way of showing our appreciation for a job well done. (133)

4

Dear Mrs. Davis:

Thank you for your invitation to address the National Life Insurance convention. I[1] would very much like to accept, but my present schedule will not permit me to attend. Perhaps I can suggest[2] someone else.

When I was in New Orleans last year, I had the opportunity to hear a fine speaker, Janet[3] Chase. Her background and accomplishments are impressive.

You can reach Ms. Chase at her home at 413 West Elm Street.[4] I think you would be completely satisfied with her as a speaker. Sincerely yours, (95)

5

MEMO TO: Professor Edwards

The president has appointed a committee to review our policy on[1] issuing federal loans to students. Would you be free to represent the School of Education on that[2] committee?

The committee will analyze our current methods of processing applications and investigate[3] new methods that might result in a more efficient system. I have a file containing background information[4] which will help you. It includes a copy of government regulations and a statement of university[5] policy. I can also provide copies of forms to be completed by applicants.

If it is convenient[6] for you, please plan to stop by my office on Tuesday or Wednesday. I think you'll find this assignment to be very[7] challenging and rewarding. (145)

LESSON

25

WORD DEVELOPMENT

aq-   *aqs*   *aq-*

rqs   *rq-*   *rq-*

lrzr-   *lrzrs*   *lrzr-*

~zr-   *~zrs*   *~zr-*

nqs   *nq-*   *nq-*

WORD CONSTRUCTION

kpzr   *lzrl*

rqm   *lrzre*

~zrm   *Dclzr*

nqe   *nqes*

Dplzr   *lrzrr*

WRITING ASSIGNMENT

1. *erp- lno lau*
ke ksl hs fon
~ rzlls vr Sde
lb v sal.

~ Sde Ncas la
ls sle, ~ fss
gro- sle w Sa.

2. *idlc l kfr la*

3. *r akN hs suq-*
lae uz · ss

n ⌒ C ∫ns db	cals etc.
⊃- qlrl nℓd ∨	
⌒ol.	5. idlc lrsv u
	bcll so ho ns
4. y uv ol qs	c rds ⌒ cℓ
ksrn r ⊃k	∨ pℓ∫ b uʒ_ u
⌒dse elb hpe	sℓ.
lsn adyl brsrs	

READING AND WRITING EXERCISES

1

Dear Mr. and Mrs. Gray:

The minute you see our guide to managing money, you'll know we designed it for you.[1] Our authors talked with people like you across the country. Their purpose was to learn ways to help people on set[2] incomes live more economically. The result is a book called *Money—How to Make the Most of It.*

Money[3] gives you a complete guide to managing your income. It shows you how to make, save, budget, and spend your earnings to your[4] best advantage. *Money* is easy to read and convenient to use. It provides everything our advisers[5] wanted and more. Planning a trip? *Money* tells you how to do it and save. Shopping for food? *Money* can reduce your food[6] bills by 40 percent.

You must see this guide to appreciate what it will do for you. Order your copy by[7] returning the enclosed form in our postage-free envelope. Send your check today and put *Money* in your home[8] planning. Yours truly, (164)

2

Dear Miss Brown:

It gives me great pleasure to invite you to this year's national convention. If you plan to attend,[1] please complete the enclosed reservation form and return it by October 2.

This year's location represents[2] our response to the results of a questionnaire sent to our members. When the membership requested a change, we[3] sent inquiries to hotels and convention centers in several major cities. We chose Columbus, Ohio,[4] because the conditions there met our requirements. Columbus also offered the best convention rates for our[5] guests.

As a member of the arrangements committee, I am making a survey. Would you prefer to hold the[6] convention in the same city each year, or would you prefer to visit different cities? Please give me your suggestions[7] in the space marked "comments" on the reservation form.

We appreciate your continued support for[8] our meetings. I look forward to seeing you again this year. Very truly yours, (174)

3

MEMO TO: Ed Parker

I am most pleased with our plans for holiday window displays. When our committee was formed,[1] we asked a representative of each department to contribute suggestions. It was rewarding to see the[2] number and range of suggestions we received.

If our plans are okay with you, we will incorporate new toys with[3] traditional items of the past. For example, we located some rare antique toys to present against a[4] background of modern paintings. We would like to acquire a system of lights and sounds to give added emphasis.

We[5] could still use our painted landscapes if we give them a new look. We might try arranging electronic games and toys[6] against the old background. As soon as you have the opportunity, won't you meet with me to discuss these suggestions?[7] (140)

4

Dear Mrs. Moore:

Thank you for your letter concerning the use of our floor cleaner. We are de-

lighted to hear that[1] the machine performed so well. We have been pleasantly surprised by the large demand for this machine. So many[2] people requested it that we have a waiting list.

In order to serve more customers, we are acquiring[3] another machine. As soon as this machine is ready for use, you may call in your reservation directly to[4] our store on Second Street. We hope the new system provides more efficient service for everyone.

We appreciate[5] your comments. I hope you will visit us often. Very truly yours, (112)

5

MEMO TO: Manager of Marketing and Sales

When the Board of Directors met last Monday, they voted to start[1] a new division to produce paper goods. This represents a major change and offers opportunities in[2] a new market.

We will distribute the paper goods through our food division. This system appears to be the most[3] economical and convenient method of handling the new merchandise.

Sales representatives who call on[4] supermarkets will increase their calls to include discount stores, drug stores, and other retail outlets which carry our[5] goods.

We anticipate using Denver, Colorado, as a test market for the new line. We will measure the[6] results of a six-month test to form future marketing plans. If we accomplish our goals in the test market, we[7] will turn our attention to national sales. (148)

LESSON
26

WORD DEVELOPMENT

[shorthand characters]

WORD CONSTRUCTION

[shorthand characters]

WRITING ASSIGNMENT

[shorthand writing assignment 1 and 2]

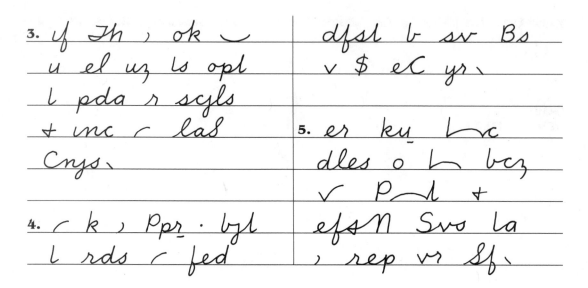

READING AND WRITING EXERCISES

1

Dear Mr. and Mrs. Cramer:

I am delighted to inform you that I have been assigned to handle your[1] policy. As you learned from his letter, your former agent was promoted to vice president. I would like to add[2] that the promotion came in recognition of his outstanding contributions to our company.

Although[3] assuming his duties will be very challenging, I plan to continue the prompt and thorough service characteristic[4] of Mr. Johnson. As a first step, I would like to meet you personally and review your policy[5] to determine that the coverage meets your current needs.

Because it is important for both of you to be[6] present during our conversation, I will call on Wednesday, May 27, to find a time convenient for[7] everyone. It will be a pleasure visiting with you. I am new to your city, and I look forward to making[8] new friends. Sincerely yours, (164)

2

Dear Mr. Wilson:

It is with great pleasure that we welcome you to our consumer club. The enclosed membership[1] card allows you to shop during regular store hours from Monday through Saturday.

Because our store is reserved[2] for the use of members only, we ask that you not invite visitors on regular shopping days. However,[3] on the first Sunday of each month, we hold an open house in which club members invite guests to learn about our club[4] and the many benefits it offers.

We now have 250 members. As our membership continues[5] to grow, we will offer even greater discounts on merchandise. At the present time, we are selling brand-name[6] items at 20 percent below the suggested retail price. You can help our membership grow by telling people[7] in your neighborhood about our program. Visit our Sunday open house and ask a friend to come with you. Sincerely[8] yours, (161)

3

Dear Melvin:

Although I have given much thought to your suggestion that I run for a seat in the House of Representatives,[1] I have decided against doing so at this time. My wife is recovering from a recent illness,[2] and her continued return to good health is our most important concern.

However, I would like to offer my[3] support to another individual who would make an outstanding representative. Sue Martin has[4] served as manager of public relations, director of consumer affairs, and assistant to the Secretary[5] of State. I feel confident she would be received well by the public.

Both my wife and I wish to thank you[6] for your kindness and encouragement. Under different conditions, I would have gladly accepted. I hope the[7] opportunity comes again in the future. Yours very truly, (152)

4

Dear Mr. and Mrs. Smith:

It gives us great pleasure to invite you to attend the private opening of our[1] new store at 301 North State Street.

Our shop will carry a full line of men's and women's clothing, from sporting goods[2] to formal wear. We have taken great care to choose your favorite brands and designs. Just as important, we are[3] providing a wide range of prices from which to choose.

Our store opens to the public on November 6. On the[4] evening before, we would like you to be our guest for a private showing in which our models will be wearing[5] original designs from New York. Following the show, we invite you to have refreshments, visit, and browse.

Please join[6] us for what promises to be an evening of fun, fashion, and surprises on Friday, November 5. Very[7] truly yours, (142)

5

Dear Mr. Stevens:

Thank you for your promptness in reporting the damages to your home.

We understand that the[1] fire damage makes it necessary for you to find other living quarters while repairs are being made. We have[2] forwarded your claim to a local agent who will help you make those arrangements.

Because your homeowner's policy[3] provides complete coverage, all repairs will be made at no cost to you. This coverage includes whatever[4] living arrangements you choose. Before we can process your claim, we will need a complete list of the individual[5] items damaged or lost. Please mail or deliver that list to your agent's office at 2100 Main[6] Street.

As your insurance company, we want to return you to your home quickly. In the meantime, please allow our[7] agent to help locate pleasant and convenient accommodations. Cordially yours, (155)

LESSON

27

WORD DEVELOPMENT

al~l-	al~ls	al~l_
ksl-	ksls	kslr
eSa	Sa-	Sam
rqSs	rqS-	rqS
akda-	akdas	akda_

WORD CONSTRUCTION

ks-	kvrsy
nkr	plzrs
rqms	kl~l
gr'	apv-
nls	~pv_

WRITING ASSIGNMENT

1. ls L , n rsp
lu nqe ab kb_
pl vu nk L .
lrS fM.

l nvr u l dl
⌐ m adrs S
~e n bSn MA.

2. / gvs ~e plzr

3. lu p sr u kMs
~ ~e zz uv

[Shorthand notes]

READING AND WRITING EXERCISES

1

Dear Executive:

You are one of the few people chosen to receive three free issues of *Business Review*.

Why?[1] Because we mail inquiries only to the individuals who meet our requirements. *Business Review* is[2] directed at informed individuals like you who have shown a concern for major problems and opportunities[3] facing our nation.

To help you decide that our magazine is right for you, we are sending you the first three[4] issues free of charge. Then you may choose to receive the six following issues at half price.

Included in those nine[5] issues will be major news stories. One issue will investigate the purchasing of corporate stocks. Other[6] articles will discuss health care, banking services, and programs for retirement.

Please watch for *Business Review* in[7] your mail. Yours very truly, (145)

2

Dear Dr. Brown:

I am pleased to recommend Dr. David Wilson for the position of vice president of[1] your university. Having known David both personally and professionally for the past five years, I[2] feel that I can comment on his character, educational leadership, and accomplishments.

David relates[3] well to people. He has provided an especially important link between industry and academic[4] affairs. David has represented our college on several committees in city and county government.[5]

Because of David's importance to our college, I would be sorry to see him leave. I also know that dedicated[6] individuals must move on to new goals in order to satisfy their own need for growth.

If you have other[7] questions regarding Dr. Wilson, I will be glad to answer them. Yours very truly, (157)

3

Dear Customer:

April 15 is quickly approaching, and we must reduce our entire stock of new and used cars.[1] That means great savings for wise shoppers. This year we will offer better discounts than ever before.

Beginning[2] February 3, we will run full-page newspaper advertisements telling the public about our low prices, but[3] we are giving you an opportunity to get ahead of the rush. We are inviting loyal customers[4] like you to take advantage of these great savings on February 2. You will find a wide range of makes, models,[5] and prices from which to choose.

You will also have every consideration in making ordinary credit[6] arrangements. Our chief credit officer will be on hand during sale hours to approve your credit.

Remember,[7] early shoppers always have the best choices. We hope to see you there. Yours truly, (154)

4

Dear Parent:

Our school dental health program is about to get underway.

As part of this program, your child will have[1] the opportunity to participate in a dental clinic free of charge. Each child will be given a free[2] toothbrush and shown how to use it properly.

Because of the importance of good home care during this program, we[3] ask all parents to help us by supervising their children's brushing habits both in the mornings and in the evenings.[4]

Please note that this program does not replace regular dental care. Although your child may be receiving regular[5] dental treatments, he or she can still benefit from participating in the classroom clinic.

This program[6] has been approved by the county dental council. If you wish your child to participate, please sign the form below[7] giving your consent. Return it to your child's teacher by October 5. Sincerely yours, (156)

5

Dear Mr. Evans:

As our valued customer, you know that our store takes pride in handling only the best in[1] gentlemen's wear. This policy has proved to be the most important reason individuals like you continue[2] to shop here.

This year we have a surprise for you. To show our appreciation for the support you have given[3] our business, we will offer a before-Christmas sale for preferred customers.

Just show our salespeople this letter,[4] and you will receive 20 percent off our regular prices—including our entire line of suits, coats,[5] shirts, and sportswear.

This is a change from past years when prices were reduced after Christmas. By shopping early, you can[6] accomplish two important goals—one for you and the other for the gentlemen on your shopping list.

We[7] cordially invite you to attend this sale and enjoy choosing from our full stock. It would give us great pleasure to serve[8] you again. Cordially yours, (165)

LESSON

28

ABBREVIATIONS

merchandise	et cetera	federal
street	question	especially
government	okay	quart
university	represent,	incorporate,
	representative	incorporated
advertise	Christmas	

BRIEF FORMS

READING AND WRITING EXERCISES

1

Dear Mr. Davis:

We will be happy to send an engineer to your home to make a complete analysis[1] of your heating and cooling system. The characteristics you described over the phone indicate that your unit[2] is very different from most of the units we see. Because it is not a common unit, we are sending[3] our chief engineer to make the analysis personally. He will plan the visit at your earliest[4] convenience and report his findings promptly.

We can then answer your questions about repairing or replacing[5] the unit. If it becomes necessary to order a new unit, the equipment will be delivered and[6] installed for the purchase price quoted to you originally.

Please call our headquarters to make arrangements for[7] the analysis. Yours very truly, (147)

2

Dear Miss Roberts:

I am writing in response to your recent letter in which you noted that late charges had been[1] added to your last monthly payment. I am happy to report those charges have been removed because we did[2] receive your payment within the time allowed.

Regarding your request to change the due date on your loan, we understand[3] your need for such a change, and we would like very much to accommodate you. However, we cannot change the[4] payment schedules currently in use. Ordinarily, all of our mortgage arrangements call for a payment on the[5] 20th of each month.

Our advice is that you make two payments within one month. If you can do this, your payment[6] would be automatically received before its due date each month.

I hope this suggestion helps. Please feel free to call[7] whenever you have questions. Cordially yours, (148)

3

Dear David:

I was pleased to learn of your recent appointment as vice president of Western University.[1] I know the search and screen committee considered many top executives before making a final decision.[2]

As dean of our college, you made many important contributions to our institution. Because of your[3] accomplishments here, we have seen increases in enrollment, improvements in teaching methods, and the start of[4] many needed programs.

We wish to invite you and your family to be our guests at a banquet to be given[5] by our staff, faculty, and student council. This is our way of thanking you for the progress achieved under your[6] direction.

In the future, we will keep you informed on what we are doing here. I hope you will do the same for[7] us. Best wishes in your new position. Very truly yours, (151)

4

MEMO TO: Fred White

May I propose a new method for recording claims in our central data processing unit?[1] I suggest that claims representatives use a stamp which indicates that the item has been reviewed and should[2] be either accepted or not accepted for processing. When a document comes to a data clerk without[3] this stamp, that item should be returned with the request that it be completed properly.

This method would require[4] very little additional effort and would result in a more efficient and convenient system for[5] everyone. (101)

5

Dear Mr. Johnson:

Thank you for responding to my resumé and letter of application for the position[1] of reporter.

I was very happy to learn that I am

under consideration for an opening[2] on your business writing staff. I will gladly send you additional examples of my writing and any[3] other information you desire.

As you requested, I asked two of my college professors to write letters of[4] recommendation. You should receive letters from Dr. Thomas Wilson and Dr. Susan Allen within a[5] few days.

Because of my background in business and economics, I feel certain I could contribute much as a[6] business reporter. Could we set up a meeting to discuss this further?

I would be happy to come to Atlanta[7] and deliver my writing examples in person. I look forward to meeting with you at your convenience.[8] Sincerely yours, (163)

LESSON

29

WORD DEVELOPMENT

rlxs	_rlx-_	_rlxy_
vprss	_vprs-_	_vprs_
vpln-	_vplns_	_vpln_
vpNs	_vpN-_	_vpN_
_v-_	_vs_	_v_

WORD CONSTRUCTION

lxs	_S_
vdNs	_vpl_
_~x_	_vlny_
vsvl	_vpy_
vpl	_Xs_

WRITING ASSIGNMENT

d hord alC-, .
cpe v . nu pln
ofr- b . sv + ln
co n lon, af rd
r brsr i fll Stn
ud N lse ,
Ph ecd uz r

pam pln ofr-,
v crs ino el
nd C inf ldl
if r pln , apo
f r co, lu ll
e no if u lc
r pln, llb gld

READING AND WRITING EXERCISES

1

Dear Ms. Edwards:

I am applying for the position of copy editor with your firm. I believe you will[1] find my background appropriate for the duties described in your newspaper advertisement. Included in the[2] enclosed resumé is a list of books I have edited. I have also written indexes, cover copy,[3] and advertising brochures. During the last four years I have emphasized studies in computer programming.

I am[4] extremely eager to meet with you and learn more about your department. Your company produces excellent[5] books which rate highly in the marketplace. May we discuss this position in person? I will call on June 23[6] to arrange an appointment at your convenience.

I look forward to talking with you then. Very truly yours,[7] (140)

2

Dear Mr. James:

We have enjoyed serving as your travel agent during the past year. We hope our services[1] resulted in many pleasant memories for you and your family. May we also take this opportunity[2] to remind you we are always ready to help with your travel plans. Whether you are looking ahead to summer[3] or just needing to make last-minute arrangements, we will gladly take care of the details.

Our full line of services[4] makes any trip easier and more relaxing for you. After cold weather sets in, why not consider some[5] fun in the sun? We have several exciting new travel packages to show you. It is not too soon to plan[6] your family outings for summer vacation. An early start ensures you choice accommodations and makes the[7] trip more fun for everyone.

We are looking forward to seeing you this coming year. Sincerely yours, (158)

3

Gentlemen:

Our shipment of office supplies arrived in excellent condition and on schedule this morning. While[1] we were checking our merchandise against the invoice, we discovered an extra order of envelopes. Although[2] we requested only 20 boxes of envelopes, we received 21. Each box contained the full amount[3] of 200 printed envelopes.

We find no mention of the extra envelopes on the invoice, but we see[4] no reason to return the extra package and will add it to our supplies. We have determined that the[5] individual unit price of each box is $8.95, and we are enclosing a check for that[6] amount.

If you feel that this matter requires further discussion, please let me know. Thank you for your promptness in[7] delivering our goods. We are more than satisfied with the attention given our order. Cordially yours, (159)

4

Dear Mrs. Arnold:

This is in response to your call informing us of the damages to your car. Would you please[1] complete and return the enclosed report within one week following the date of your accident? Please be certain[2] to record all necessary information. Use the additional space provided to explain how the[3] accident occurred.

Your claims account number is 07-5151. Our regional claims manager[4] will call on you promptly to examine the damage and approve arrangements for making repairs.

We recommend[5] an excellent body shop near you which handles most of our claims. We suggest this firm only because it rates[6] highly in customer satisfaction. Whether you choose this specific shop or another firm is entirely up[7] to you.

Please call if you have any further questions. Yours truly, (152)

5

Dear Mr. and Mrs. Hastings:

The accounting firm of Davis and Davis wishes to welcome you to Buffalo.[1]

As new residents, no doubt you are finding much to learn about our city. We hope the enclosures in this[2] letter help. We included a map of the city and other information designed to help you feel at home[3] in your new location.

May we tell you about our firm? Davis and Davis is the oldest accounting firm in[4] this city. We think the main reason we have so many customers is the prompt and loyal service we offer[5] both businesses and individuals.

We hope you will allow us to handle your accounting needs. As your tax[6] representative, we can do everything—record information, compute taxes, and complete the forms for you.[7] We will mail you a note near the end of the year to remind you of our service. In the meantime, don't hesitate[8] to call on us. Yours very truly, (167)

LESSON
30

WORD DEVELOPMENT

WORD CONSTRUCTION

WRITING ASSIGNMENT

READING AND WRITING EXERCISES

1

Dear Policyholder:

The insurance benefits described in the attached bulletin bring many improvements[1] to your existing program.

Our new medical plan covers long hospital stays and medical leaves from your job.[2]

In order to help you better understand your new insurance plan, we are enclosing a bulletin containing[3] complete details. Please study it. We encourage you to discuss the new program with your personnel officer[4] soon. Use this individual meeting as an opportunity to ask questions about your coverage.[5] It is important that you fully understand the program in order to use it to your best advantage. Yours[6] truly, (121)

2

Gentlemen:

We are happy to tell you we have found the solution to the problem in your engine. After[1] making a complete investigation, our research manager discovered that the problem was caused by a short in[2] the electrical system of the engine. We have replaced the wiring, and your engine is running well. We are[3] confident you will experience no more problems.

We can deliver and install the unit next week. Can you[4] accept delivery on May 7?

Your engine is under warranty, so the repairs will be made free of charge. It[5] will be necessary, however, to present a claim form. Please forward the claim at your earliest convenience.[6]

We are glad to be of service. Yours very truly, (130)

3

Dear Mr. Stevens:

This is just a reminder to let you know you may now file an exemption on your state[1] property taxes. In order to take advantage of this opportunity, you must file by March 1.

If you have[2] not had experience with filing for a mortgage exemption, you will find the process to be quite easy. Take[3] the enclosed form to your county tax assessor. The entire process takes approximately 15 minutes to[4] complete and will result in a major savings against next year's taxes.

May I emphasize again the importance[5] of filing by March 1. Although the exemption applies to next year's taxes, it must be filed this year.

Please call[6] on me whenever I can be of help. Cordially yours, (130)

4

Dear Mr. Edwards:

Accompanying this letter is the report you requested presenting long-range plans for[1] our marketing division. The figures represent an item breakdown of gross sales, costs, and percentage of[2] profits over the last five years.

Sales increased sharply in the southern and western regions of the country. Except for[3] two states, sales reached record highs in these regions and represented 40 percent of our total sales last year.

I[4] am also presenting a five-year marketing plan based on past sales and projections for the future.

The overall[5] picture is a pleasant one. I hope the plan meets with your satisfaction. Very truly yours, (117)

5

MEMO TO: Marketing and Sales Personnel

We are pleased to add two new members to our staff. Mr. Harold Smith[1] and Ms. Betty Madison joined our division on July 15.

Both of these people assume the position[2] of regional manager for equipment sales and service. Harold will cover the northeast part of the country,[3] and Betty will cover the West Coast.

Harold spent nine years in the U.S. Air Force as chief engineer in charge of[4] the testing program. Betty has managed sales programs in California, Washington, and Oregon.

Betty[5] is already operating out of her office in San Francisco, and Harold will be moving into his[6] Boston office immediately. Please join me in welcoming these exciting new people to our company.[7] (140)

LESSON

31

WORD DEVELOPMENT

klc-	klcs	klc_
Pjcs	Pjc-	Pjcr
afc-	afcs	afc_
nspcs	nspc-	nspcr
crc-	crcs	crc_

WORD CONSTRUCTION

lrß	clc
aplcß	rznß
slc-	rjc
rspc	efcs
cßq	kflß

WRITING ASSIGNMENT

d M hnre alc- r   fl ⁀ld. crNl a

r cpes und.   lgl dcms r b_

bcz r fls v grn   cpl n r lgl ofs.

so lry + r uz-   ⁀n und. il⁀

b so me ppl ∕ ·   · fl clrc lb gld

nes luz · dfrN   lgl ⁀ fu. ls

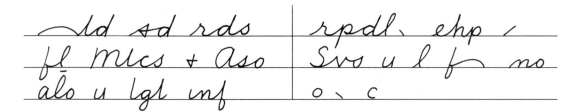

READING AND WRITING EXERCISES

1

Dear Miss Barnett:

Thank you for the outstanding training sessions you put together this week. The instruction was[1] excellent and should be of great benefit. Please express our appreciation to everyone who helped make such[2] a pleasant experience for us.

The program made such a strong impact on our staff that we wish to plan a[3] similar event for next year. We expect to have approximately 200 people eligible for the[4] program. Would you consider bringing your training group to our city?

We would follow your efficient timetable. By[5] starting the meetings promptly at 8:30 a.m. and ending at 5 p.m., we could complete the sessions in[6] three days. If you approve, I will begin making arrangements now. We already have some suggestions in mind.

I[7] look forward to your reply. Again, you have our thanks for a job well done. Very truly yours, (156)

2

Dear Ms. James:

Thank you for promptly reporting the loss of your charge card. As I explained during our phone conversation,[1] our computer registered the loss at the time you made the call. That prompt action is espe-cially important[2] for your protection. You are no longer responsible for purchases made by anyone other than authorized[3] persons.

The enclosed cards contain new account numbers. If you have additional copies of your old cards on[4] hand, please dispose of them now. The new cards are in effect now and are the only cards authorized for your account.[5]

We are always happy to be of help. Cordially yours, (110)

3

Dear Mark:

On behalf of the parents at Smith School, I wish to thank you very much for the excellent program you[1] conducted at last month's meeting.

Your comments regarding the school board's recent action came at an appropri-ate[2] time. For those of us who did not understand the details of the new program, your explanation helped a great deal.[3]

Many of us would like to enroll our children when they become eligible. We can plan now for the future.[4]

May I emphasize again, Mark, how much we appreciated your willingness to come on such short notice. As[5] they indicated by their responses after the program, the other parents also benefited from your[6] important remarks. I hope it was a rewarding experience for you as well. Sincerely yours, (138)

4

Dear Mr. Brown:

Have you considered opening a trust account with our bank?

Trust accounts offer many[1] advantages to people in the middle-to-high income range. They provide a long-term savings plan which can be used[2] for different purposes. For example, a trust fund for your children protects their future. As the account grows,[3] it becomes a basis for their college education, or it can fund another investment to give them an[4] especially sound start in life.

There are excellent tax benefits accompanying trust funds. We would be happy[5] to explain them in detail. Why not make an appointment today to learn how these plans operate?

We offer[6] many services designed to help with family and estate planning. We hope you will take advantage of some[7] of the options that are available, Mr. Brown. Very truly yours, (152)

5

Dear Mr. Smith:

Although your payment which was due September 1 has not been received, we are pleased to tell you that[1] your policy has been kept current through our automatic loan provision. This has resulted in a slight[2] increase in the size of your loan. Please note that the attached statement records this latest action.

As we have explained in[3] the past, it is to your advantage to repay the loan as quickly as possible. By doing so, you renew[4] the full value of your policy. When you make a payment, please return the attached statement with your check. Please write[5] your policy number on the check to help us process your payment quickly.

May we also remind you that we[6] are always happy to answer questions and help in any way we can, Mr. Smith. Do not hesitate to call[7] our toll-free number at any time. Cordially yours, (150)

LESSON

32

WORD DEVELOPMENT

⁓ps	⁓p-	⁓pm
scr-	scr_	scr ˡ
ddcs	ddcℬ	ddcℬ ˡ
kc-	kcs	kc_
su-	suℬ	suℬ ˡ

WORD CONSTRUCTION

kn ˡ	cps ˡ
Psnl ˡ	q𝓜ᶫˢ
lcl ˡ	els ˡ
nss ˡ	Pbℬ ˡ
elℊℬ ˡ	psℬ ᶫˢ

WRITING ASSIGNMENT

ꜰ з ⌐ hd v ls hsp ⁓ lr Cldrn, ꝑnl
iз hpe lhr la · sC · arm Pvds ·
nu Cldrns unl gr bnfl l ⌐ prⁿⁿs
, l̩ Ppz-, з pl v ls зlз ⌐ psⁿⁿs, ldl
Ppzl prⁿⁿs lb alo- · nd f ls unl ·
l rⁿm hr wr hsp Sva з ⁓d ⁓ lcl

rzd Ms, ✓ lol Sva- 80% ‿ n fvr ✓ ls unl, yfl hpe + prod lse ls ‿dr fnll

rsv ‿ all ⁄ nds, z mbrs ✓ hsp brd ul no dol ‿s lrsv · ʃ rpl o ls nu pln, vlu

READING AND WRITING EXERCISES

1

Dear Mr. Webster:

This is to confirm our phone conversation concerning the contract you already have with[1] James Brown.

As I indicated earlier, Mr. Brown has decided to resell the property and has[2] employed me to make the arrangements for him. The proposed new owners wish to purchase his equity and assume the[3] basic contract now in effect.

Please note that the following changes are to be made: The new loan rate[4] will replace the rate paid originally. We will start over with a new ten-year term.

Please ask your attorney to[5] draw up the new agreement with these changes. We will review it before closing. If the agreement requires a[6] title search, the new owners will accept that responsibility.

I appreciate your help in completing[7] the new contract. Yours truly, (145)

2

Dear Mrs. Allen:

Thank you for your letter, copies of the contract, and related legal information[1] concerning the sale of the property. I was delighted to hear that the closing took place as scheduled without[2] questions or difficulties of any kind.

I wish to call your attention to the enclosed copies of correspondence[3] canceling our original fire insurance policy on that house. I have not yet received anything[4] from the new owners indicating that they have taken out a new policy. Would you be able to determine[5] that adequate coverage has been arranged?

I am also returning your copy of our agreement which[6] we signed as you requested. I assume you can now record the deed and consider the contract completed.

Thanks[7] again for your help. Cordially yours, (146)

3

Dear Ed:

I am pleased to say I will be visiting Tulsa even sooner than we expected.

I plan to bring[1] our new sales managers on a trip through our western plants during the week of March 6. I want to show them our[2] excellent facilities and the programs currently in effect. We will arrive on flight 519 at[3] 5:30 p.m. on Wednesday. Could you meet us and have dinner with us that evening?

I would appreciate meeting[4] Thursday morning with you, our new employees, and anyone else you think they should meet.

If it is not too difficult[5] to arrange, Ed, I would like our guests to go through all of the plants. We might consider the possibility of[6] renting a bus for Thursday afternoon. What do you think? Your opinions always contribute greatly to our efforts.[7]

We plan to leave at about 9 o'clock the next morning. Your help is certainly appreciated. Sincerely,[8] (160)

4

Dear Ms. Adams:

This letter is in response to your recent inquiry regarding apartment rentals. Although[1] we have no apartments available now, we anticipate openings within the next three months. I encourage[2] you to keep checking with us.

We do require a security deposit in the amount of a full month's[3] rent. This deposit will be returned after your furnishings have been removed and an inspection shows that no[4] damages have occurred. We also request 30 days' notice when you plan to move from the apartment.

You may choose[5] a one-year or two-year lease. The two-year contract offers the advantage of saving approximately[6] $20 per month in rent. Each unit contains complete laundry and kitchen facilities.

We will be happy to[7] show you an apartment. Call our rental office to set up an appointment. Sincerely yours, (156)

5

Dear Mr. Wilson:

Here is the report you requested. As you can see, your earning power is your most important[1] asset. We agree that your life insurance policy should provide for the educational and daily[2] needs of your family in the event of your death.

What does it take to meet these goals? We recommend that your[3] insurance offer benefits of up to six times your present earnings.

I suggest you purchase a 20-year term[4] policy in the amount of $250,000. The table on page 7 lists the benefits[5] and costs of this specific plan. If you wish to purchase the policy, simply complete and return the enclosed[6] application.

Thank you for allowing us to advise you, Mr. Wilson. Very truly yours, (138)

LESSON 33

WORD DEVELOPMENT

nB	ƠB	uB
rboN	uboN	boNre
bNs	bN	ubN
cvr-	cvr_	ucvr
ll	l'	ul_

WORD CONSTRUCTION

ulc	urznB
uern-	uld-
ucl	ul8-
udvd-	u—p-
udu	ulk

WRITING ASSIGNMENT

mo l ⌐yr v bys ⌐r │ scl splis lb Ɵpla-
el ofr sv_ v bln │ bln ⌐ bys + grls dpls,
20 + 30 % o a bc=l= │ el ac pam w f⌐
scl nds = cll_ zlz │ v c4 cr crds + Psnl
splis. a cll_ 4db │ Ccs. loz Psns ⌐4 l
⌐rc- don 20%. a │ c4 parl Ccs 4db

[shorthand notation]

READING AND WRITING EXERCISES

1

MEMO TO: Marketing Staff

Our show this year was the best we have ever had. Our products made a favorable[1] impression, and we received many compliments after the show.

We also received some suggestions. For example,[2] many dealers are of the opinion that a 60-day delivery time is too long. It should be reduced[3] to 30 days. If at all possible, we will make that change within the next few months.

Among the compliments[4] received were those referring to our display of cameras connected to computer terminals. We had[5] approximately $1,000,000 worth of merchandise there.

Our employees also made a good impression. Our[6] sincere thanks go to an outstanding staff for an exciting show. (131)

2

Dear Mrs. Clark:

I want you to know that I have become a senior account agent for National Life,[1] Inc.

As of May 1, I will move to a new location at 819 South State Street, where I will[2] continue to give you personal service whenever you need it.

In order to bring your policy up to date,[3] I have enclosed a questionnaire asking for specific information. Would you please return the form in the[4] postage-free envelope provided?

Please note that my telephone number (555-3100)[5] remains unchanged. Until May 1, you can visit me at my present office. If you have questions, I hope you[6] will call. When you are in the neighborhood, stop by. My assistant and I are always glad to talk with you. Yours[7] very truly, (142)

3

Dear Reader:

We have already sent several bills for our magazine, *Art News,* ordered in your name. So far we[1] have not received any payment or explanation.

It is not our custom to ask for payments with orders. We[2] think our readers appreciate the convenience of being able to make payments whenever they settle their[3] other household or office accounts. We consider our readers to be informed individuals who accept[4] responsibility for contracts they have made.

We know that there is a good reason for your delay in making[5] payment. It will take only a few minutes to settle this matter—either with a check or a few words explaining[6] the delay. Please return your response with the invoice in the accompanying envelope. Sincerely yours,[7] (140)

4

Dear David:

Thank you for the opportunity to recommend my assistant manager, Jennifer Young, for[1] the position of public relations director. I do so with pleasure.

Jennifer has many fine qualities[2] representative of good management. One strong point is her ability to express her opinions both in[3] speech and in writing. She shows an understanding of company goals along with a sincere concern for our[4] other employees.

Jennifer assumes full responsibility for any job, no matter how difficult.[5] Until she came to the advertising department, Jennifer had no experience in management.[6] Nevertheless, she supervised several projects in the manner of an experienced department head.

In my[7] opinion, Jennifer is ready for increased responsibility. She will bring many fine qualities to the[8] position under consideration. Yours truly, (169)

5

Dear Customer:

We are converting your billings to a new electronic data processing system which will[1] serve you more efficiently. Here are the basic changes affecting your loan payments:

1. As of[2] January 1, we will employ the use of the enclosed payment book.

2. Your new monthly due date will always be the[3] first day of each month. If your payment was due on January 10, it is now due on January 1. It will[4] be due the first day of every month thereafter.

3. If your payments are automatically deducted from your[5] checking or savings account, you will not receive a payment book.

These changes will enable us to process your[6] payments more promptly. If you have questions, please call the banking office nearest you or our customer service[7] department. Cordially yours, (144)

LESSON 34

WORD DEVELOPMENT

insls	insl-	insll
ssls	ssll	sslz
spsls	spsll	spslz
dvs	dv-	dvms
acq-	acqs	acqms

WORD CONSTRUCTION

krsl	rzdnsl
ofsll	sqnsl
esnsl	dvr
fnnsll	aso-
plnsll	kq-

WRITING ASSIGNMENT

d snlr rln z | dfe ls gsln bl, ls
uno s mbrs vr | bl d alo coo ldl
grp vb nvlv- n. | lr o ras, / d Aso
fu l Pvn ncrss n | Pvd nu plses f lca
yl + gsln ras, e | yl o prps nr c se,
nvr u l hlp b vo l | loz nu plses cdb

[shorthand notation]

READING AND WRITING EXERCISES

1

Dear Paul:

I wish to express my support for the new bonus system officially adopted at the departmental[1] meeting. Our sales personnel have devoted much time to developing a demand for our product, and the[2] results have been excellent. As our market coverage continues to grow, orders increase accordingly.[3]

After presenting the new policy at our regional sales convention, I received many calls from sales[4] personnel concerning points they found confusing. In order to prevent misunderstandings, I plan to issue a[5] memo right away explaining the policy in detail. As an initial step, I am organizing a[6] meeting with all sales managers to go over each point. Would you be able to join us next Friday at 10 a.m.?[7]

All in all, the proposal has been well received in the field. I expect to see even greater success in[8] national sales. Sincerely yours, (166)

2

Dear Dr. Williams:

It gives me great satisfaction to recommend Dr. Elizabeth Carter for the rank[1] of associate professor. As support for this action, I offer the attached file containing a summary[2] of her experience. I am also including two articles she recently published, along with opinions[3] of students and other faculty.

Elizabeth joined our staff three years ago. She has developed new[4] courses in American history which have contributed much to our program. She shows a regard for high[5] teaching standards and provides an excellent example for students and other faculty.

Elizabeth is[6] a teacher with great potential and a promising future. It seems only appropriate that we acknowledge[7] her contributions with this promotion. Very truly yours, (151)

3

Dear Mrs. Clark:

I would like to thank you for meeting with me on Monday to discuss my employment search. Although[1] I had acquired some literature on how to approach potential employers, your advice was of special help.[2] I now appreciate more fully the importance of making a good impression, and I have a better[3] understanding of how to accomplish that goal.

I am following your advice and writing individual[4] letters of application to send with each copy of my resumé. I also appreciate the resumé[5] you gave me. I am developing my own resumé with more ease and success than I had expected. As[6] a result of our meeting, I now feel that I can make that initial contact with a confident and[7] professional image.

Thank you again for your help. Yours truly, (150)

4

Dear Mr. Parker:

Thank you, Mr. Parker, for completing our questionnaire concerning the social security[1] reform bill. Here are some results from that survey:

1. The majority of people surveyed[2] (82 percent) rely upon extra income to maintain their standard of living.
2. The main source[3] of income after retirement comes from group plans provided by employers and labor organizations.[4] Other sources listed were personal business or property, insurance dividends, and personal savings.[5]
3. Most people agreed that social security benefits alone are not sufficient to meet financial[6] demands imposed by inflation.
4. Approximately 33 percent stated that a new program should be[7] developed to replace the existing plan.

Thank you again for participating in the survey. Yours truly,[8] (160)

5

Dear Mr. Davidson:

Congratulations are in order for you and your family. Your name has been selected[1] for the next volume of *Young People in America*, a very special publication.

This distinguished[2] book lists individuals under the age of 40 who are earning outstanding recognition. It cites the[3] successes of young people in all walks of life—business, industry, education, government, sports, law, and[4] medicine.

The enclosed data sheet specifies personal and professional information to be included[5] in our next volume. Please read and return the information with any corrections you wish to make.

Again,[6] congratulations on receiving this special award. Cordially yours, (133)

LESSON

35

ABBREVIATIONS   volume   literature   America, American

BRIEF FORMS

a	*pv*	*⌣*
ks	*nx*	*nl*
yp	*ar*	*apx*
ß	*opn*	*dfc*
kc	*~p*	*sd*
dv	*og*	*aso*
acy	*suc*	*kq*

READING AND WRITING EXERCISES

1

Dear Sir:

Here are four reasons why you should keep reading.

1.   You are an educated person.
2.   You know a bargain[1] when you see it.
3.   You believe in saving money when you can.
4.   You know how to take advantage of a[2] rare opportunity.

If you need a fifth reason, consider this. You are among only 100 people[3] to receive this offer. As part of a rare marketing program, you and 99 others have been selected[4] to try our vacation homes.

Village Homes is a planned neighbor-hood already under construction. It is perfect[5] for young families. Village Homes has everything you will want and more. When you see the contracts that are available,[6] you will probably say you can't afford not to buy!

Let us prove it. Enjoy one free night and form your own[7] opinions. To make your reservation, return the enclosed note. But hurry—the offer ends next month. Reserve your[8] date immediately. Cordially yours, (167)

2

Dear Ms. Roberts:

I am happy to accept the position of executive secretary with your firm. I[1] consider it a challenge to be the person chosen for the responsibilities you described.

I would be[2] delighted to begin employment on May 21 as you requested. Unfortunately, our school does not[3] end until May 25. May I begin the following Monday, May 28, promptly at 8 a.m.?

I[4] look forward to this opportunity to learn, grow, and build new skills. I feel certain the position will bring many[5] new and exciting experiences.

Thank you for making this opportunity possible. Unless I[6] hear differently, I will report to your office on the morning of May 28. Cordially yours, (139)

3

Dear Mr. Baxter:

Thank you for your inquiry. I believe the enclosed literature will answer your questions.[1]

Every distributor employs a full-time supervisor who makes sure that our personnel are fully trained in[2] servicing our electronic typewriters. Our distributors set up training sessions for staff, dealers, and[3] customers approximately three times per year.

Every distributor is equipped with the machinery and test[4] equipment needed to repair our machines. If it does become necessary to order parts from the factory,[5] those orders are processed and shipped immediately.

If you would like further information, Mr. Baxter,[6] please contact me again. We feel our training is of value not only to new employees but also to[7] continuing personnel as well. We are always glad to answer your questions. Sincerely yours, (156)

4

Gentlemen:

It is that time of the year when we put away matters of the office to share personal[1] experiences with family and friends. As a contract customer, you already know that our station[2] continues its 24-hour programming during the Christmas holidays. In order to allow our employees[3] as much personal time as possible, we alter our advertising and programming schedules for a few days. From[4] 8 p.m., December 23, until 8 a.m., December 26, we will provide taped programming. All[5] advertising to be broadcast between those dates should be delivered to our offices by 5 p.m., December[6] 20, to allow sufficient time for preparation.

May we also take this opportunity to thank you[7] for your patronage. We have enjoyed serving you during the past year and look forward to continuing our[8] relationship. Cordially yours, (166)

5

Dear Friends:

When our group meets again next month, we will welcome Shelley Clark as guest speaker. The meeting is being moved[1] back one week to March 8. Shelley was unable to attend on the day regularly scheduled for the meeting.[2]

Shelley is well recognized in our city. She has headed many important committees. Most recently she[3] was elected president of the Chamber of Commerce.

Shelley comes to us immediately following a[4] trip abroad, and she brings exciting news. Traveling on behalf of our city, Shelley met with approximately[5] 45 corporations. Although the mission was a long and difficult one, it produced excellent results.[6] We have already received word that one company plans to send a representative here to investigate[7] building a new plant.

Please note the change on your calendars and plan to be present for the meeting. Very[8] truly yours, (162)

LESSON
36

WORD DEVELOPMENT

ac-	ac_	acN
syc-	sycs	syc_
as8-	as8	as8N
s⌐l-	s⌐ls	s⌐l_
acrd-	acrd_	acrdN

WORD CONSTRUCTION

CN	kfdN
dNl	r⌐N
evdN	PfN
n8N	s8d
fnN	sk

WRITING ASSIGNMENT

d⌐s jcsn lqf asr   ⌐ ol Pbl⌐ iv h,
l ⌐ L. ⌐ bclls u   obln_ dla f⌐ cos
sN l grl hlp ⌐e   lca- ol v lon. ol v
n du_ . rSC ppr   . lol v 7 iv hrd
du ls l⌐, i alspa   f⌐ ol 4. ⌐ no
fn⌐ ⌐ ppr n 2 ⌐cs.   ⌐a f rsps f⌐ ⌐

r—n 3 bf alz r | rsv . cpe v ~l
fnl rzlls, ul Stnl | fns- rpl . ul

READING AND WRITING EXERCISES

1

Dear Mrs. Smith:

We have reserved an efficiency apartment for you in Long Beach. The apartment has an[1] excellent view of the ocean and all of the facilities you requested.

Since your vacation falls during the[2] busy season, we recommend that you confirm your reservation. It would be wise to call one week in advance.[3]

Please send a $50 deposit now to reserve this apartment. If you wish us to handle all arrangements[4] for you, we will be happy to forward your check. We will also confirm the dates of your stay.

We feel certain[5] that you will enjoy living in this charming apartment on the beach. Thank you for allowing us to assist you[6] in making your travel plans. Cordially yours, (128)

2

MEMO TO: All Department Heads

Please note that university budget meetings will begin early next year. It[1] is important that you submit your proposed budgets by January 6. Initial meetings will begin[2] immediately. Final approval is scheduled for the end of April.

Because of large cuts in state allowances,[3] you should make every effort to reduce expenses. Since no new funding is available, it will be[4] impossible to begin new programs. I know that you are all doing your best to keep expenses down.

Many of[5] you have asked about pay increases. We are suggesting a standard 7 percent increase for all personnel.[6]

Any additional requests for funding must be reviewed before April 1. We appreciate your help in[7] providing your budget requests as soon as possible. (150)

3

Dear Sir:

I read with appreciation your initial issue of *Business Review* and wish to order three[1] subscriptions to be given as Christmas gifts. I am enclosing the names and addresses for your use.

I wish to[2] take advantage of your Christmas discount. I am enclosing a check for the total amount of[3] $35.85. This should cover all handling fees.

As I understand it, you will mail a greeting[4] card announcing the gift. Will the card arrive before Christmas? Please send me confirmation that the gift cards have been mailed.[5] Thank you very much. Yours truly, (105)

4

Dear Senior:

In a few weeks you will put away final exams and begin a new life.

To acknowledge the[1] importance of this event, we have asked Mr. David Cox, Secretary of State, to deliver our commencement[2] address. To our delight, Mr. Cox has accepted.

In his brief term in office, Mr. Cox has proved to be an[3] outstanding leader. We feel fortunate to have this opportunity to hear him. We hope he will share his dreams[4] for a new beginning among nations.

This is the last letter I will write to most of you. As your university[5] president, I wish to congratulate you and thank you for your support. May you be rewarded with the[6] best of health, a stimulating career, and the satisfaction of accomplishment. Above all, enjoy your new[7] life. Sincerely yours, (144)

5

Dear Mrs. Baxter:

We would like to remind you that your account is past due. Would you take a minute now to mail[1] us a check?

From time to time, we all overlook a payment. Since you have always paid your bills on time, we are certain[2] this delay must be the result of an oversight. If there is some other reason why we have not heard from[3] you, would you drop us a note of explanation?

Perhaps we should point out again that you will save money by[4] submitting your payments in advance. When your payment arrives late, a fee is charged against the unpaid balance.

Thank you[5] for your attention to this matter. If your payment is already in the mail, please disregard this notice.[6] Sincerely yours, (122)

LESSON

37

WORD DEVELOPMENT

obyc-	*obycs*	*obycv*
efcs	*efcv*	*efcvl*
ac-	*acq*	*acv*
ᴄos	*ᴄo-*	*ᴄos*
clcs	*clcq*	*clcv*

WORD CONSTRUCTION

Pdcvˡ	*Plcv*
acvˡᵒ	*dfcv*
efcv´	*sNv*
nf~	*ᴄol*
alrcv	*ᴄosp*

WRITING ASSIGNMENT

d ~rs gbsn r sms | Pbl ᴄa vb cz- b
vb arv̠ af ᴄ du da. | r rsN ᴄv. r L
r Ma pcq z du ঠ | v Ap 2 asc- u l
3d b z rsv- ঠ 9l. | dla ᴄ Ma sm l
r Jn + Jl sms arv- | e gl sil- ᴄr
nrl 2 ᴄcs la, ls | nu bld̠. Ph e dd

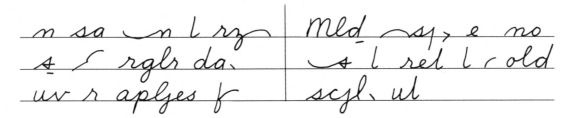

READING AND WRITING EXERCISES

1

MEMO TO: All Department Managers

As usual, each of you will be asked to prepare a performance report[1] on individual employees. However, this year's report will be different. As you can see from the[2] attached copy, we will ask employees their opinions regarding their work productivity, job satisfaction,[3] and career goals.

Please encourage your people to complete these reports as accurately as possible. Be[4] certain that everyone understands the purpose of the report—that it is to help each person achieve his[5] or her goals.

The results of these reports will have a significant effect on future planning. By working[6] together we will increase the efficiency of our organization. (133)

2

Dear Mr. Sharp:

I certainly enjoyed reading the manuscript, *New Developments in Word Processing*. Thank you[1] for allowing me to see the study in advance. I am pleased to offer my opinions on its effectiveness.[2]

I consider this work to be a significant contribution to the field. Mr. Evans gives us an[3] unusual look at the future and its impact on office procedures. As he stated in the first chapter,[4] his objectives are to survey standard equipment in use today and describe products soon to be available.[5]

Mr. Evans is selective in his choice of examples and brief in his descriptions. I found the writing[6] to be clear, well organized, and effective.

Again, I appreciate the opportunity to work with you[7] in reviewing this study. Please call on me if I can be of further help. Cordially yours, (157)

3

Dear Ed:

Now that all testing is complete, we are authorizing the release of a new product. Effective[1] immediately, we will manufacture engines for small aircraft as well as the appropriate installation[2] equipment.

We received official notice this morning to release the product for the North American market.[3] Please change your records to show the following corrections. We added a new support system and assigned a new[4] code number to reflect the change in pricing.

Orders will be shipped within a maximum of 60 days. We may[5] see a slow start in sales due to problems in the aircraft industry. However, we expect significant[6] increases during the first 18 months. We hope to lead the market within five years.

Please let me know if you have[7] any questions. Sincerely yours, (146)

4

Dear Charge Customer:

When is a winter sale not just an ordinary sale? When you see our discount prices, you[1] will know. We rarely offer savings like these. Then we make them available only to very special people[2]— our charge customers.

This is not an advertised sale. It is a personal invitation to our regular[3] customers to enjoy special benefits. Please consider it our way of saying thank you for your patronage.[4]

Choose from our top manufacturers— early American, traditional, and contemporary collections.[5] Join us for coffee and browse through our new art displays. You could be the winner of a prize to be given[6] away each day.

Shop at one of our convenient locations today and save. Remember that cash is not necessary.[7] Your signature will reserve the items of your choice. Sincerely yours, (154)

5

Dear Henry:

We recently invited an expert on writing business letters to teach a course in our plant.

She[1] stressed that a good letter is direct and brief. The information should be well organized. Watch for unnecessary[2] comments. These can distract the reader.

I was impressed by her advice to keep the tone of our letters positive.[3] We can even say no in a positive way.

You can see that I found this course to be extremely important.[4] Would you like to hear more about such a course for your office?

I would be happy to refer you to the instructor.[5] I firmly believe that we can all benefit from such instruction. Very truly yours, (117)

LESSON
38

WORD DEVELOPMENT

WORD CONSTRUCTION

WRITING ASSIGNMENT

READING AND WRITING EXERCISES

1

Dear Mrs. Davidson:

Thank you for notifying us promptly about the items taken from your car on[1] September 5 at approximately 3:30 p.m.

After we examined your policy, we determined[2] that your coverage provides a $150 deductible for losses such as you describe. There[3] are exceptions to the deductible, but they usually concern damages resulting from natural[4] causes. Your losses cannot be classified among them.

Our records show that the total value of the items[5] taken was $178. Therefore, we are enclosing a check for $28. If[6] you have further questions regarding this matter, please feel free to call at any time. We are always ready to[7] explain your policy and give you the best protection offered by it. Cordially yours, (156)

2

Dear Dr. Jeffries:

I benefited greatly from the information covered in your accounting class and[1] also

from the outside projects we completed. I am pleased to say that I have already been able to apply[2] some of that knowledge. For three months I have been working part time in the office of a certified public accountant.[3] I have assisted in classifying financial data as part of my responsibilities there.

I[4] am now preparing a resumé and letters of application. Since you are well qualified to comment on[5] my educational background, may I list your name as a reference? Your recommendation would be very[6] helpful. Very truly yours, (125)

3

Dear Mrs. Gregory:

Here is the booklet you requested, "Caring for the Patient at Home." We hope you[1] find the publication informative and useful.

May we also remind you of the full health care service we[2] now offer? We carry a complete line of health care equipment for use in the home. You can rent any item[3] with no deposit required. You pay only that part of the expense not covered by your insurance. In most[4] cases, your insurance pays for everything, and the rental equipment costs you nothing.

If you have questions about[5] your coverage, discuss them with our professional staff. They are specialists in filing medical claims and will be[6] happy to give you assistance.

Come to the experts for convenient service and the best of professional care.[7] When quality counts, you can count on us. Yours truly, (150)

4

Dear New Employee:

Welcome to World Electronics. In the enclosed envelope you will find three items of value[1] on your new job.

The first is your employee identification card. Please add your signature and carry[2] the card during regular working hours. Be prepared to show your card when you come into or leave the building.[3]

The second item is your health benefits booklet. Read it carefully. If you have any questions regarding[4] your hospital or dental coverage, call our personnel office immediately.

The third item, your[5] employee handbook, provides a complete guide to our company's services and policies. Please become familiar[6] with our procedures during your first week on your new job.

If you have any questions, don't hesitate to call on[7] us at any time. Sincerely yours, (147)

5

Dear Mr. Edwards:

Your name was suggested to me because of your research in classifying rare plants. Would you[1] please assist us in making an identification of the enclosed leaf?

My class has been collecting leaves[2] during the past two weeks. One of my students brought in this leaf. It is not shown in any of the books in our school[3] library. After we made a careful search of the literature in the county library, we found the[4] enclosed photograph that looks exactly like our leaf. As you can see, both leaves have the same unusual shape. However,[5] the plant in the picture grows in the western states and could not possibly grow this far east. Or could it?

We hope[6] you can identify our discovery. This class project has become a significant learning experience[7] for everyone. Very truly yours, (146)

LESSON 39

WORD DEVELOPMENT

ntn-	ntnr	ntnm
ns-	nss	ns_
nds-	ndss	nds_
nvus	nvu-	nvu_
est-	ests	estm

WORD CONSTRUCTION

nfr	sfkl
nvn_	nvl
ndcj	sa_
sf pvm	amr
sfdfn	klr

WRITING ASSIGNMENT

dros fs u nu cr crd, enc- + erp- l lk u z. G K, u cr lnt, sn s lp v ls L, r alC- brsr gvs r inf u rqs- ab r rz bss + ol plns la db apo f, rn chl. r aso rfs u l. lcl dlr l m u a q f hlp u u sp lnscp

[shorthand outlines]

READING AND WRITING EXERCISES

1

Dear Miss Johnson:

Did you know that you are looking at the most powerful credit card in America?

The[1] American Charge Card shown here is more than a credit card. It is your ticket to the world of international[2] business travel. You will find it accepted in major establishments all over the world.

If you wish to apply[3] for membership, simply complete the enclosed form and return it in the self-addressed envelope. If you apply[4] by Monday, May 6, you will receive an executive travel case. This special introductory gift is[5] beautifully styled to organize your personal items.

Why not put your signature on the most useful card[6] in America? Travel in the self-assured manner of experienced business people who are in control[7] and leave the rest to us. Yours truly, (146)

2

Dear Mr. Evans:

I read with interest your report presenting long-term goals for the college. May I join you in[1] pursuing some of the goals you mentioned? I propose that we arrange a meeting with potential board members.

We[2] might invite the local superintendent of schools along with people from business and industry.

We should meet[3] often to discuss academic programs. How shall we identify the needs of our community? What[4] resources are available to us? You could probably suggest many more questions.

If you agree with this[5] sample plan, I will go to work on it immediately. Would you please send me a list of people you[6] particularly wish to involve? Yours very truly, (129)

3

Dear Ms. Allen:

Thank you for your interest in the accounting firm of Davis and Davis. Your work experience,[1] educational background, and academic achievements are very impressive.

We do have an opening[2] for an administrative assistant. Your general office skills indicate that you would be highly qualified[3] for this position. Would you be willing to come in for an interview? This position could be an excellent[4] introduction to your career.

If you wish to discuss this opportunity further, please call my office[5] to arrange an interview. I look forward to talking with you. Very truly yours, (116)

4

Dear Mrs. White:

Thank you for your payment of $40. We have credited it to your account.

We especially[1] appreciate your taking the time to explain why your payments have been late. Your offer to bring the account[2] up to date in June certainly will be satisfactory.

We think we know how the misunderstanding developed[3] concerning your unpaid balance. Perhaps you did not know that you missed your January payment. When you sent[4] a double payment in March, we applied it to your January and February installments. This meant that[5] you have been one month behind. Every payment since then has been applied to the month before.

If you are still puzzled,[6] please let us know. We are always interested in improving customer service. Sincerely yours, (139)

5

Dear Mr. Baker:

Yesterday I had the pleasure of meeting an interesting and highly qualified[1] applicant for a position with our firm. I am delighted to say that Ms. Joyce Young is now an employee in[2] our data processing department.

I was impressed by the resumé she sent in advance of the interview.[3] After I had talked with her in person, I knew at once that she would be right for our organization. She has[4] an excellent background in office administration, and she presents herself as a capable and self-assured[5] employee.

I offered Ms. Young the position at the conclusion of the interview, and she called this morning[6] to accept. We are grateful to you for referring her to our firm and hope that future circumstances will[7] allow us to return the favor. Very truly yours, (150)

LESSON
40

WORD DEVELOPMENT

digs	dig-	dig_
relz-	relzs	relz_
cra-	cras	cra_
evlas	evla-	evla_
grja-	grjas	grja_

WORD CONSTRUCTION

idas	vluy
nul	apliN
Cul	beN
rnul	sres
siN	liβl

WRITING ASSIGNMENT

d r hrve ι N	adj l r knˡ , ⌐
l kplm u б kpʃ	mbrs ✓ sle ksl
vu nu bld sιl-	r pln_ · rbn = cl_
o prҫ drʋ , r sle	sr ⌐ me б da u
cl prod ✓ ls nu	rqδ-, ⌐ pl , nvι-

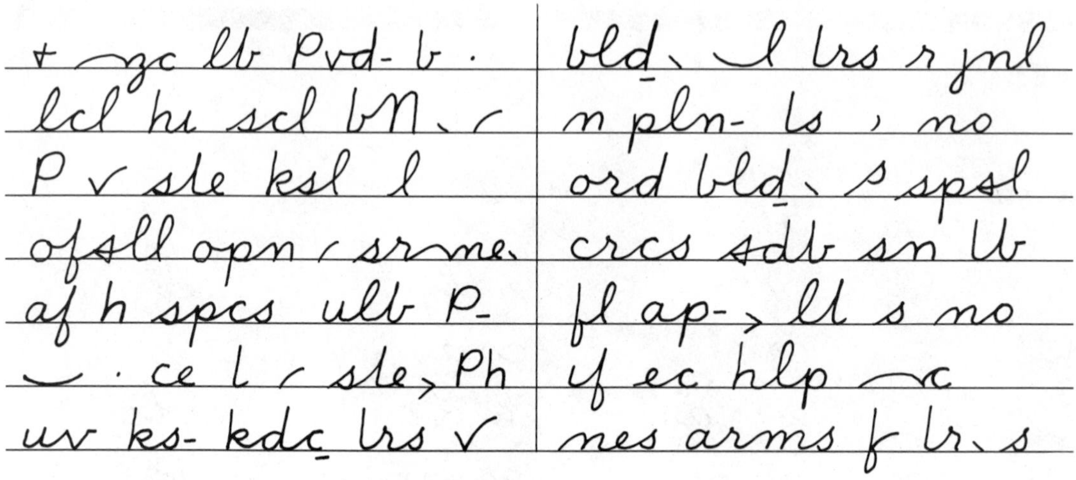

[Shorthand notation spanning two columns]

READING AND WRITING EXERCISES

1

Gentlemen:

Please send me any literature you have about recreation areas in your state.

I am[1] planning our annual family vacation. We are particularly interested in hotels or[2] apartments located on the beach. Do you have brochures listing rooms available in a middle price range?

We have[3] also heard many good things about your state parks. Please include a catalog describing the parks, their facilities,[4] and the activities provided by each one.

Are there special circumstances we should know about? Are[5] conditions in your area suitable for camping? What is the busy season for your parks?

We would be grateful[6] for any advice you have toward helping us plan a successful vacation. We look forward to hearing from you.[7] Sincerely yours, (144)

2

Dear Ms. Allen:

If you are like most homemakers, you spend much of your day preparing meals. Shouldn't you have the best[1] possible materials to work with? We think you should. That is why we created our new line of cookware.

We[2] are so convinced of the quality of our product that we make this money-back guarantee. Order your special[3] introductory set and use it on a trial basis. Make your decision at the end of a 30-day[4] period. If you are not completely satisfied, you may return the set. We will then return your money.

What[5] makes us so sure you will love our cookware? We have been manufacturing fine products for over 40 years, and[6] we know what good cooks look for. Once you try this particular set, you will never want to use anything else.

Prove[7] it to yourself. Treat yourself to something special in the kitchen. Cordially yours, (154)

3

Dear Mr. Miller:

Thank you for offering me the position of audio-visual director of your[1] advertising agency.

I am pleased that you admire my work. I certainly enjoyed meeting you at the[2] convention last month, and it is very tempting to accept your offer. However, I am not ready to leave my[3] work here. I have begun some new programs, and I would like to make sure that they are firmly established and under[4] control before I leave. I am sure you understand.

You are to be congratulated on your creative work[5] in radio and television. It would be a challenge and a pleasure to work with you. I hope this[6] opportunity will be possible again sometime in the future. Sincerely, (134)

4

Dear Michael:

Many fine suggestions have been made for our next area sales meeting. We can expect to see[1] several new faces because of recent additions in personnel. Therefore, I believe a review of our[2] basic program would be especially helpful. It has also been suggested that we distribute sample copies[3] of all company literature. Such literature would include catalogs, sales brochures, and customer handbooks.[4]

I am recommending that all personnel attend our next area sales meeting. These meetings have proved to[5] be very valuable, and I would like to schedule more of them. Perhaps it would be in everyone's best[6] interest if we were to hold similar sessions at the end of each period. I will be eager to hear what[7] you think. Very truly yours, (145)

5

Dear Elizabeth:

The agenda for next month's area sales meeting is now complete. On the first day a[1] member of our sales staff will provide the program review you requested. We will then allow the rest of the morning[2] for a question-and-answer period. Specific changes in existing products will be discussed during the[3] afternoon session. At this time it would be appropriate to distribute any new literature you have[4] regarding changes in pricing, advertising, or distribution.

The second day will be devoted entirely[5] to the presentation of new products. Our advertising department is preparing the new brochures which[6] will provide an exciting addition to our existing literature.

I would be grateful for any[7] suggestions you may have. Cordially yours, (146)

LESSON
41

WORD DEVELOPMENT

ac_	ac_	Tac
plNs	plN-	TplN
rla	lal	Tla
rf	kf	Tf
pl	pl	Tpl

WORD CONSTRUCTION

Tl	Tqlz
Tf-	TSrs
TS	Tpz
Tfr-	Tql
Tac	T

WRITING ASSIGNMENT

drs le w evN er asc_ u l kb l r
v · dN nvlr s, fN drv, e Nr
n u fl ud N egpm l cor l
hlp l arv l. Sds crc v ol sles
r sle, n nd v nu r sz v rs. ncrs-
ryN e egpm + dms f us vr lx $

[Shorthand notes]

READING AND WRITING EXERCISES

1

Dear Mr. Ames:

Thank you for your inquiry about transferring your current automobile insurance to a[1] different car. The process is quite simple. In order to do so, just give me the model, year, make, and registration[2] number of your new car. I will take care of everything else.

There will be a slight increase in your annual[3] premium. The amount of the increase will depend on the kind of new car you purchase. Please notify me[4] as soon as you buy your new car. Becoming effective immediately, the change in your new policy will[5] provide you with continued coverage. I will mail you a copy of the revised policy for your signature.[6]

Here is good news. Effective Tuesday, July 1, you will receive a reduced rate reserved for drivers who have[7] not experienced an accident over a five-year period. This is our way of rewarding safe driving[8] habits.

We are always ready to be of service. Very truly yours, (173)

2

Dear Committee Members:

You are all wonderful! Please accept our congratulations for making this year's fund drive[1] the biggest and best ever.

We reached our goal two weeks ahead of time. When the drive ended on October 4,[2] we had exceeded all expectations.

While there are no material rewards associated with volunteer[3] work, we know you share our feelings of achievement and satisfaction. We wish to thank everyone who helped in[4] preparing radio and newspaper advertisements, in providing transportation, and in making hundreds[5] of calls.

You helped to make this drive a success, and we are grateful to you for putting your abilities to work[6] for us. Yours very truly, (125)

3

Dear Ms. Evans:

The enclosed real estate contract has been revised to meet the terms we agreed upon. Please note on[1] the attached diagram that the new property line has been clearly defined. It can no longer be confused with[2] surrounding areas. Copies of this revision were delivered to the new owners yesterday, and they gave[3] it their immediate approval.

After adding your signature to all three copies of the contract, you will[4] need to return them to me. Once you have signed the forms, the contract becomes final. The title to your property[5] is then transferred to the new owners.

You have my congratulations on handling this matter so well. A[6] transaction such as this ordinarily takes several weeks. This matter has been resolved quickly and conveniently[7] because of the help of everyone involved.

I hope you will call on me again if I can be of assistance.[8] Cordially yours, (163)

4

Dear Jeffrey:

Could you please prepare a new list of all companies we are currently supplying? Because we wish[1] to add information, the format may differ from the one you have followed in the past. We ordinarily[2] group all customers by size of account. However, our marketing department produces a similar[3] document listing all customers by the area served. It would be more efficient to create one list that is[4] equally beneficial to both departments.

Why don't you meet with our marketing

director to establish[5] a new format? Please continue to show the dollar amount received from each customer on an annual[6] basis. It would also be helpful to give an item breakdown of the products purchased.

As a source of vital[7] information, your final copy of the list will indeed prove to be valuable. Sincerely, (156)

5

Dear Sir:

Our agency has been authorized by the federal government to prepare a report on transportation[1] services. We will be surveying and sampling cities with 100,000 or more residents. Your[2] city qualifies, but we are interested in having you participate for reasons other than size.[3] Your administration has become known for its modern ideas and leadership. Because we consider your[4] community to be extraordinary, we are asking you to serve as a model for our study.

The enclosed[5] form asks for detailed information. Please return it by the date specified. Could you also supply us with[6] literature on your transportation companies? We would like to know about schedules, fares, and the number of[7] clients using the services on a daily basis.

As soon as the results have been published, we will mail[8] individual copies to all participating cities. Sincerely yours, (174)

LESSON
42

ABBREVIATIONS   establish   superintendent

BRIEF FORMS

[shorthand symbols]

READING AND WRITING EXERCISES

1

Dear Ms. Jackson:

Our request for funds has been approved. To serve our city and surrounding area, we can now[1] establish our proposed leadership program. I am sure you understand the social significance of this program.[2] Clients chosen to participate will be trained in leadership methods. Once the clients have completed our course,[3] they will be encouraged to direct other similar programs in our community.

Our objective now is[4] to locate an experienced person to lead our training sessions. We believe you to be the most qualified[5] person because of your achievements in volunteer work. Would you be willing to serve as president?

Of course, you[6] will wish to give this matter careful consideration. Please allow me to answer any questions you may have[7] at this time. Sincerely, (145)

2

Dear Mr. Wilson:

Your announcement came as wonderful news. Such a program is certain to be successful in[1] this community. Did I understand correctly that a grant has been awarded for this project? The grant itself[2] is quite an accomplishment. Congratulations go to you and the other individuals who submitted[3] the proposal.

I would be happy to serve on your board of directors, but I cannot accept the position[4] of president. The administrative duties would require more time than my present circumstances allow.[5] However, I can think of several people who have made significant contributions in volunteer work.[6] Would you like me to recommend those who might be interested in becoming president?

I feel pleased to be[7] considered for this position. Thank you for your vote of confidence. Cordially yours, (156)

3

Dear Betty:

A few weeks ago you expressed interest in working for our company. At that time we had no[1] openings to offer you. Since circumstances have changed, I can now refer you to a position which became[2] available only yesterday.

I am enclosing a job description for the office of administrative[3] secretary. All applicants must have previous experience in office work and skill in shorthand[4] to qualify for this position. As I recall, you have already established an impressive background which[5] includes writing and transcribing shorthand proficiently.

If you wish to apply, please call my office by Friday[6] afternoon. We can then arrange an interview to discuss the position further. Yours very truly, (139)

4

Dear Mr. Roberts:

I have a question regarding our usual procedure for paying insurance claims for[1] medical visits.

We ordinarily advise the employee to present the form for the doctor's signature[2] during the visit. In some cases, the doctor requests additional time for entering information[3] relative to that visit. The form is then mailed to the employee, and the employee submits it to our office.[4]

This procedure adds several days between the time the employee pays for the visit and the date the form[5] arrives in our office. Once the forms come in, we process them immediately and issue a check to the[6] employee. By that time, however, the total transaction has taken up to three weeks.

There must be a way to save[7] processing time. I would be grateful for your ideas on this subject. Yours truly, (155)

5

MEMO TO: All Employees

Pamela Carlson will become general manager of our manufacturing[1] division as of July 1.

When the change becomes effective, the manufacturing division will be[2] expanded to include two new departments. The office of industrial research will be responsible for[3] long-range planning, and a systems control department will ensure continued excellence for our product. You will be[4] hearing more about both of these developments in the near future.

Having joined our staff as an engineer,[5] Pamela brought many fine ideas to our operation. She has acted as superintendent for special[6] projects, and most recently she has served as worldwide analyst in our international division.

I am[7] sure Pamela will welcome your assistance in getting established in her new office. She is looking forward[8] to working with each of you. (165)

SPELLING STUDY

All employees who write business communications need to spell correctly frequently used words. In fact, the ability to spell well consistently ranks among the traits most desired by employers.

Surprisingly, a large number of spelling errors occurs from a relatively small number of words. Each of the six Spelling Checks that follow consists of 100 common words that tend to cause spelling problems. Mastery of the words in the Spelling Checks will enable you to spell correctly most of the words in which spelling errors frequently occur. Although the lists are not long, time devoted to the spelling study of the words on each list will certainly be time well spent.

SPELLING CHECK NUMBER 1

1. ability	26. congratulations	51. interest	76. pursuant
2. access	27. consumer	52. irrelevant	77. questionnaire
3. accounting	28. cooperation	53. lease	78. receipts
4. acknowledgment	29. counseling	54. liability	79. recommend
5. adaptable	30. curriculum	55. lose	80. referring
6. admissible	31. definitely	56. marriage	81. repetition
7. advise	32. determine	57. meant	82. restaurant
8. allotted	33. disappoint	58. merge	83. salary
9. alternative	34. distribution	59. modifications	84. security
10. analyze	35. edition	60. necessary	85. sewer
11. applicants	36. eligible	61. objectives	86. sincerely
12. approximate	37. enrollment	62. offered	87. software
13. ascertain	38. especially	63. opinion	88. stationary
14. assure	39. exaggerate	64. organization	89. subject
15. audit	40. executive	65. parallel	90. sufficient
16. ballot	41. expenses	66. participation	91. surprise
17. believable	42. facilities	67. percentage	92. taxable
18. brilliant	43. fascinate	68. personally	93. termination
19. calendar	44. filed	69. physical	94. through
20. capacity	45. foreign	70. possibility	95. transmitted
21. categories	46. general	71. preliminary	96. truly
22. changeable	47. growth	72. presently	97. union
23. clients	48. human	73. prior	98. usually
24. commitment	49. incidentally	74. professional	99. valve
25. competitor	50. installation	75. proprietary	100. versus

SPELLING CHECK NUMBER 2

1. abrupt	26. conscientious	51. issue	76. pursue
2. accessible	27. continuing	52. juvenile	77. quotient
3. accrual	28. coordinator	53. led	78. receive
4. acquaintance	29. courses	54. library	79. recommendations
5. addition	30. customer	55. mailable	80. registration
6. admittance	31. delegate	56. material	81. replacement
7. advisory	32. develop	57. media	82. retrieval
8. allowable	33. disastrous	58. microcomputer	83. schedules
9. among	34. district	59. monitoring	84. seize
10. anxious	35. education	60. nickel	85. shining
11. appointment	36. embarrass	61. obsolete	86. specifically
12. aptitude	37. entered	62. officer	87. stationery
13. assessed	38. essential	63. opponent	88. subsequent
14. athlete	39. exceed	64. orientation	89. suggested
15. authorization	40. exhibit	65. parcel	90. survey
16. bankruptcy	41. experience	66. particularly	91. technical
17. believe	42. facility	67. perform	92. than
18. brochure	43. field	68. personnel	93. throughout
19. campus	44. forty	69. plausible	94. transportation
20. capital	45. generally	70. practical	95. university
21. category	46. guarantee	71. premises	96. utilization
22. choose	47. imagine	72. prevalent	97. variable
23. closing	48. incompatible	73. privilege	98. vice
24. committee	49. institution	74. professor	99. warranty
25. complaint	50. internal	75. provided	100. whose

SPELLING CHECK NUMBER 3

1. absence	13. assessment	25. compliance	37. entitled
2. accidentally	14. attendance	26. conscious	38. established
3. accumulate	15. authorized	27. continuous	39. excellence
4. acquire	16. banquet	28. corporate	40. existence
5. address	17. beneficial	29. courteous	41. explanation
6. adolescent	18. brought	30. debatable	42. facsimile
7. affect	19. cancellation	31. delinquent	43. finally
8. allowed	20. carried	32. development	44. friend
9. amounts	21. ceiling	33. discuss	45. government
10. apologies	22. chose	34. divide	46. handicapped
11. appraisal	23. collateral	35. effect	47. immediately
12. argued	24. committees	36. emphasis	48. increase

49. instruction
50. international
51. issued
52. knowledge
53. ledger
54. license
55. maintenance
56. mathematics
57. medical
58. miniature
59. moral
60. ninth
61. occasion

62. omission
63. opportunity
64. original
65. parity
66. passed
67. performance
68. persuade
69. pleasant
70. practice
71. premium
72. previously
73. probably
74. projects

75. providing
76. pursuing
77. rapport
78. received
79. recommended
80. relieve
81. representative
82. rhythm
83. scheduling
84. sense
85. similar
86. specifications
87. stockholder

88. substantial
89. suggestions
90. surveyor
91. techniques
92. their
93. together
94. treasurer
95. unnecessary
96. utilized
97. varies
98. video
99. weather
100. withdrawal

SPELLING CHECK NUMBER 4

1. abundance
2. accommodate
3. accurate
4. acquisition
5. adequate
6. advantageous
7. affluent
8. almost
9. analyses
10. apologize
11. appreciable
12. arguing
13. assistance
14. attention
15. available
16. basis
17. benefited
18. bureaus
19. candidate
20. cashier
21. census
22. cite
23. column
24. communications
25. conceive

26. consensus
27. contractors
28. correspondence
29. criteria
30. decision
31. describe
32. different
33. discussed
34. divine
35. efficient
36. employee
37. entry
38. estate
39. excellent
40. exists
41. extension
42. faculty
43. financial
44. fulfill
45. governor
46. hardware
47. implementation
48. indicates
49. insurance
50. interpret

51. it's
52. labeling
53. legible
54. limited
55. manageable
56. matrix
57. medicine
58. minimum
59. morale
60. nominal
61. occasionally
62. omit
63. opposite
64. paid
65. partial
66. password
67. permanent
68. persuasive
69. plotter
70. precede
71. preparation
72. primitive
73. procedures
74. prominent
75. provisions

76. pursuit
77. realize
78. receiving
79. reconcile
80. reluctant
81. required
82. ridiculous
83. secretaries
84. separate
85. specified
86. strength
87. substantially
88. summary
89. susceptible
90. technology
91. then
92. toward
93. tries
94. until
95. validate
96. variety
97. villain
98. warehouse
99. weird
100. writing

SPELLING CHECK NUMBER 5

1. academic	26. controlled	51. laboratory	76. reason
2. accomplish	27. council	52. leisure	77. recent
3. achieve	28. criticism	53. loneliness	78. reference
4. across	29. deductible	54. manufacturing	79. remittance
5. adjournment	30. description	55. maximum	80. requirement
6. advertisement	31. disability	56. mentioned	81. role
7. all right	32. disease	57. miscellaneous	82. secretary
8. already	33. division	58. mortgage	83. sequential
9. analysis	34. either	59. noticeable	84. site
10. apparent	35. employees	60. occurred	85. speech
11. appreciated	36. environment	61. omitted	86. studies
12. argument	37. estimated	62. optical	87. succeed
13. associated	38. except	63. participant	88. supersede
14. attorneys	39. expenditure	64. pamphlet	89. system
15. beginning	40. extraordinary	65. past	90. temporary
16. benefits	41. familiar	66. permissible	91. there
17. business	42. fiscal	67. pertinent	92. tragedy
18. cannot	43. function	68. position	93. useful
19. cassette	44. grammar	69. preferred	94. valuable
20. certainly	45. height	70. prepared	95. various
21. claimants	46. implemented	71. principal	96. visible
22. coming	47. industrial	72. proceed	97. whether
23. comparative	48. integrated	73. property	98. wholly
24. concern	49. interrupt	74. psychology	99. written
25. consistent	50. itinerary	75. quantity	100. yield

SPELLING CHECK NUMBER 6

1. accelerate	15. balance	29. currently	43. family
2. accordance	16. behavior	30. defendant	44. follows
3. achievement	17. binary	31. despair	45. further
4. activities	18. businesslike	32. disappear	46. grateful
5. administrative	19. capabilities	33. diskette	47. heroes
6. advisable	20. casualty	34. dissatisfied	48. important
7. allotment	21. certificate	35. document	49. initial
8. alter	22. clientele	36. electrical	50. intelligence
9. analyst	23. commission	37. enclosing	51. inventories
10. appearance	24. competitive	38. equipped	52. its
11. appropriate	25. conference	39. evaluate	53. laid
12. arrangement	26. consultant	40. excess	54. letterhead
13. assumption	27. convenience	41. expense	55. loose
14. audio	28. counsel	42. extremely	56. marketable

57. means
58. menu
59. misspell
60. notify
61. occurrence
62. operating
63. optimism
64. paragraph
65. participate
66. patient
67. personal

68. phase
69. possession
70. prejudiced
71. prescription
72. principle
73. production
74. proposal
75. purpose
76. quarter
77. reasonable
78. recognize

79. referred
80. renewable
81. resolution
82. safety
83. sector
84. services
85. situation
86. station
87. studying
88. successful
89. supervisor

90. tariff
91. terminal
92. thorough
93. transferred
94. undoubtedly
95. using
96. valuation
97. vendor
98. volume
99. while
100. wholesale

READING RATE (words per minute)

Words in Letter	80	90	100	110	120	130	140	150	160	170	180	190	200
82	1:01	0:55	0:49	0:45	0:41	0:38	0:35	0:33	0:31	0:29	0:28	0:26	0:25
84	1:03	0:56	0:50	0:46	0:42	0:39	0:36	0:34	0:31	0:29	0:28	0:27	0:25
86	1:04	0:57	0:52	0:47	0:43	0:40	0:37	0:34	0:32	0:31	0:29	0:27	0:26
88	1:06	0:59	0:53	0:48	0:44	0:41	0:38	0:35	0:33	0:31	0:29	0:28	0:26
90	1:08	1:00	0:54	0:49	0:45	0:42	0:39	0:36	0:34	0:32	0:30	0:28	0:27
92	1:09	1:01	0:55	0:50	0:46	0:42	0:39	0:37	0:34	0:32	0:31	0:29	0:28
94	1:10	1:03	0:56	0:51	0:47	0:43	0:40	0:38	0:35	0:33	0:31	0:30	0:28
96	1:12	1:04	0:58	0:52	0:48	0:44	0:41	0:38	0:36	0:34	0:32	0:30	0:29
98	1:13	1:05	0:59	0:53	0:49	0:45	0:42	0:39	0:37	0:35	0:32	0:31	0:29
100	1:15	1:07	1:00	0:55	0:50	0:46	0:43	0:40	0:38	0:35	0:34	0:32	0:30
102	1:16	1:08	1:01	0:56	0:50	0:47	0:44	0:41	0:38	0:36	0:34	0:32	0:31
104	1:18	1:09	1:02	0:57	0:52	0:48	0:45	0:42	0:39	0:37	0:35	0:33	0:31
106	1:19	1:11	1:04	0:58	0:53	0:49	0:45	0:42	0:40	0:37	0:35	0:33	0:32
108	1:21	1:12	1:05	0:59	0:54	0:50	0:46	0:43	0:40	0:38	0:36	0:34	0:32
110	1:23	1:13	1:06	1:00	0:55	0:51	0:47	0:44	0:41	0:39	0:37	0:35	0:33
112	1:24	1:15	1:07	1:01	0:56	0:52	0:48	0:45	0:42	0:40	0:37	0:35	0:34
114	1:25	1:16	1:08	1:02	0:57	0:53	0:49	0:46	0:43	0:40	0:38	0:36	0:34
116	1:27	1:17	1:10	1:03	0:58	0:54	0:50	0:46	0:43	0:41	0:38	0:37	0:35
118	1:28	1:19	1:11	1:04	0:59	0:54	0:51	0:47	0:44	0:41	0:40	0:37	0:35
120	1:30	1:20	1:12	1:05	1:00	0:55	0:51	0:48	0:45	0:43	0:40	0:38	0:36
122	1:31	1:21	1:13	1:07	1:01	0:56	0:52	0:49	0:46	0:43	0:41	0:39	0:37
124	1:33	1:23	1:14	1:08	1:02	0:57	0:53	0:50	0:46	0:44	0:41	0:39	0:37
126	1:34	1:24	1:16	1:09	1:03	0:58	0:54	0:50	0:47	0:44	0:42	0:40	0:38
128	1:36	1:25	1:17	1:10	1:04	0:59	0:55	0:51	0:48	0:45	0:43	0:40	0:38
130	1:38	1:27	1:18	1:11	1:05	1:00	0:56	0:52	0:49	0:46	0:43	0:41	0:39
132	1:39	1:28	1:19	1:12	1:06	1:01	0:57	0:53	0:49	0:47	0:44	0:42	0:40
134	1:40	1:29	1:20	1:13	1:07	1:02	0:57	0:54	0:50	0:47	0:44	0:42	0:40
136	1:42	1:31	1:22	1:14	1:08	1:03	0:58	0:54	0:51	0:48	0:46	0:43	0:41
138	1:43	1:32	1:23	1:15	1:09	1:04	0:59	0:55	0:52	0:49	0:46	0:44	0:41
140	1:45	1:33	1:24	1:16	1:10	1:05	1:00	0:56	0:53	0:49	0:47	0:44	0:42

Words in Letter	80	90	100	110	120	130	140	150	160	170	180	190	200
142	1:47	1:35	1:25	1:17	1:11	1:06	1:01	0:57	0:53	0:50	0:47	0:45	0:43
144	1:48	1:36	1:26	1:19	1:12	1:06	1:02	0:58	0:54	0:51	0:48	0:45	0:43
146	1:50	1:37	1:28	1:20	1:13	1:07	1:03	0:58	0:55	0:52	0:49	0:46	0:44
148	1:51	1:39	1:29	1:21	1:14	1:08	1:03	0:59	0:56	0:52	0:49	0:47	0:44
150	1:53	1:40	1:30	1:22	1:15	1:09	1:04	1:00	0:56	0:53	0:50	0:47	0:45
152	1:54	1:41	1:31	1:23	1:16	1:10	1:05	1:01	0:57	0:54	0:51	0:48	0:46
154	1:56	1:43	1:32	1:24	1:17	1:11	1:06	1:02	0:58	0:54	0:51	0:49	0:46
156	1:57	1:44	1:34	1:25	1:18	1:12	1:07	1:02	0:59	0:55	0:52	0:49	0:47
158	1:59	1:45	1:35	1:26	1:19	1:13	1:08	1:03	0:59	0:56	0:53	0:50	0:47
160	2:00	1:47	1:36	1:27	1:20	1:14	1:09	1:04	1:00	0:56	0:53	0:51	0:48
162	2:02	1:48	1:37	1:28	1:21	1:15	1:09	1:05	1:01	0:57	0:54	0:51	0:49
164	2:03	1:49	1:38	1:29	1:22	1:16	1:10	1:06	1:02	0:58	0:55	0:52	0:49
166	2:05	1:51	1:40	1:31	1:23	1:17	1:11	1:06	1:02	0:59	0:55	0:52	0:50
168	2:06	1:52	1:41	1:32	1:24	1:18	1:12	1:07	1:03	0:59	0:56	0:53	0:50
170	2:08	1:53	1:42	1:33	1:25	1:18	1:13	1:08	1:04	1:00	0:57	0:54	0:51
172	2:09	1:55	1:43	1:34	1:26	1:19	1:14	1:09	1:05	1:01	0:57	0:54	0:52
174	2:11	1:56	1:44	1:35	1:27	1:20	1:15	1:10	1:05	1:01	0:58	0:55	0:52
176	2:12	1:57	1:46	1:36	1:28	1:21	1:15	1:10	1:06	1:02	0:59	0:56	0:53
178	2:14	1:59	1:47	1:37	1:29	1:22	1:16	1:11	1:07	1:03	0:59	0:56	0:54
180	2:15	2:00	1:48	1:38	1:30	1:23	1:17	1:12	1:08	1:04	1:00	0:57	0:54
182	2:17	2:01	1:49	1:39	1:31	1:24	1:18	1:13	1:08	1:04	1:01	0:57	0:55
184	2:18	2:03	1:50	1:40	1:32	1:25	1:19	1:14	1:09	1:05	1:01	0:58	0:55
186	2:20	2:04	1:52	1:41	1:33	1:26	1:20	1:14	1:10	1:06	1:02	0:59	0:56
188	2:21	2:05	1:53	1:43	1:34	1:27	1:21	1:15	1:11	1:06	1:03	0:59	0:56
190	2:23	2:07	1:54	1:44	1:35	1:28	1:21	1:16	1:11	1:07	1:03	1:00	0:57
192	2:24	2:08	1:55	1:45	1:36	1:29	1:22	1:17	1:12	1:08	1:04	1:01	0:58
194	2:26	2:09	1:56	1:46	1:37	1:30	1:23	1:18	1:13	1:08	1:05	1:01	0:58
196	2:27	2:11	1:58	1:47	1:38	1:30	1:24	1:18	1:14	1:09	1:05	1:02	0:59
198	2:29	2:12	1:59	1:48	1:39	1:31	1:25	1:19	1:14	1:10	1:06	1:03	0:59
200	2:30	2:13	2:00	1:49	1:40	1:32	1:26	1:20	1:15	1:11	1:07	1:03	1:00